Praise for
GRIT IT DONE

Reid Tileston has taught me that to be a better citizen means to be a better entrepreneur. And the best way to do that is by owning things, not running them. This is the guide to true entrepreneurial success we've all been waiting for: a primer on buying, growing, and selling businesses you can be proud of. He doesn't cut any corners or pull any punches. He grits it done—and shows us how to do the same.

Jeff Goins
Wall Street Journal bestselling author of *Real Artists Don't Starve*

In *Grit it Done*, serial entrepreneur Reid Tileston takes you on the entrepreneur's journey showcasing the resilience, perseverance and hustle it truly takes to run your own business. But Reid doesn't just tell - he shows you how it's done by offering actionable advice and down-to-earth strategies on developing the right mindset to help you defy the odds and move you past those inevitable barriers to success.

Craig Wortmann
Clinical Professor of Marketing, Founder of Sales Engine,
Founder & Academic Director of the Kellogg Sales Institute

Finally, a realistic view of ETA. Reid's emphasis on "grit" and "on-the-ground" work hits the bullseye. I have worked with dozens of searchers - many have an overly romantic view of being an owner-operator and don't understand the daily muck, mess and trauma of running a SMB. Reid brings this reality into clear view and, more importantly, provides perspectives and tools to help owner-operators be successful. All while still conveying the thrill of success and fulfillment that is possible.

Steve Morrissette
Serial Entrepreneurship Through Acquisition Investor & Coach,
Professor-University of Chicago Booth School of Business

Reid is one of a kind. His tenacity and sticktoitiveness are on full display in this valuable glimpse into small business ownership. It is a worthy addition to the growing body of knowledge for aspiring entrepreneurs through acquisition.

Mark Anderegg
Entrepreneurship Through Acquisition Investor, Successfully Exited Operator, and Professor at Dartmouth Tuck School of Business

Buying and building a small business is a powerful way to create meaningful work with significant financial return potential. This book provides a master class on how to execute on a search in an advantaged way. Get started today!

Brian Wolfe
Entrepreneurship Through Acquisition Investor and Professor, Washington University in St. Louis Olin School of Business

Reid Tileston's *Grit It Done* is a masterful roadmap for aspiring entrepreneurs eager to navigate the trenches of acquiring a business. As an exited CEO and investor, so much of this book resonates with me. As Reid says, "Be Like (Abraham) Lincoln: treat failure as a building block of success." Leading a small business is a constant struggle to overcome a litany of setbacks and Reid's passion to help navigate that journey is incredibly inspiring. Unlike so many business books, this is a very practical read and offers a window into the entrepreneurial spirit of small business success.

GJ King
Entrepreneurship Through Acquisition Investor, Successfully Exited Operator, and Professor at Case Western Reserve University

An insightful, practical and implementable approach to buying, running and successfully exiting an entrepreneurial venture. In our ever-evolving business landscape, *Grit it Done* stands out as a beacon of practical wisdom for aspiring and seasoned entrepreneurs alike.

Leonard Lane
Professor of Strategy, University of California Irvine, Paul Mirage School of Business

Grit It Done is a good read that shines light into the world of small business ownership. A useful guide for those looking to become business owners as well as those who are looking to take their business to the next level. As a Professor and business owner myself, I can attest that there is a lot of wisdom in his writings and Reid's passion for the topic is clear.

Simon Peck
Associate Professor, Department of Design & Innovation,
Weatherhead School of Management

Owning and operating a small business is a great frontier of freedom. It allows you to do something you enjoy, provide for yourself, and do a lot of good for others. However, new startups are difficult, and the failure rate is high. Buying a business is a great solution. Reid Tileston has written a beautiful book on how to find, close and operate an existing company. Everyone looking at entrepreneurship as a future career needs to read it.

Mike Glauser
Executive Director, Center for Entrepreneurship,
Huntsman School of Business, Utah State University, Successful Entrepreneur

Grit It Done is a great addition to the emerging field of Entrepreneurship Through Acquisition. Reid Tileston has produced a book that is instructive, inspirational and a guide for those that have any entrepreneurial DNA and are looking to use that to buy and scale a business.

It will be invaluable to those wishing to understand the landscape more or become an ETA entrepreneur. Reid's passion for the topic and interest in helping others to follow his path is obvious. As an educator and business owner this is a highly recommended read.

Dr. Camelia Clark
Owner Paradise Memorial Funeral Home

With small business being the backbone of the economy, Reid's insights and suggestions can help those with the desire to succeed realize their dreams. Applying the principles taught an entrepreneur will see how to capitalize on what's working and more quickly modify the weakness turning them into strengths. A great read for the entrepreneurial minded.

Russel McSweeney
Managing Member The McSweeney Group

Powerful, Actionable and Inspiring. *Grit It Done* delves into the essence of perseverance and determination. This book came as a refreshing read that speaks to the heart of an entrepreneur with practical case studies, stories and examples that will help any current or aspiring entrepreneurial business owner learn the necessary skills to think, assess, act, and respond to any business opportunity. A must read!

AJ Vaden
Co-Founder + CEO, Brand Builders Group

Grit it Done provides a comprehensive journey through the world of entrepreneurship through acquisition. Packed with practical frameworks and actionable steps, it is the ultimate resource for aspiring business owners. From initial assessment of readiness to execution of a successful exit, this guide covers it all. Reid's personal anecdotes add a memorable touch, offering invaluable insights into the real-world application of the book's principals. A must-read for anyone dreaming of acquiring and operating their own business. Reid's expertise transforms concepts into actionable lessons, making the path to business ownership clear and achievable.

Denise Shade
Managing Member, Cormmitto Partners

I highly recommend this book to aspiring entrepreneurs seeking a firsthand perspective on the entire journey of searching, acquiring, operating, and exiting through acquisitions. Whether you're a novice or an experienced professional, this book offers valuable insights and guidance for success in the world of entrepreneurship through acquisitions.

Subayu Mandal
Entrepreneurship Through Acquisition Practitioner

Reid's guidance and the wealth of information provided have been instrumental in shaping my understanding of entrepreneurship through acquisition. The practical approach to strategic planning, due diligence, and overcoming challenges in the acquisition process has proven to be incredibly insightful.

Shawn Stypa
Owner, Pring Roofing

Thanks to Reid's guidance, I have gained invaluable insights and a deeper understanding of being a business owner. These learnings have not only contributed to my academic growth but have also equipped me with practical skills that I am confident will serve me well in my future endeavors.

David Donnelly
Managing Partner, EIA Capital

Case Dismissed… small business ownership wins! If you are interested in business ownership, read this book. If it speaks to you, it will show you specifically how to get on the ownership path NOW. It makes the case for small business ownership and the opportunity it provides to create a huge difference for you and your community.

Scot Lowry
Professor, Case Western Reserve University and
Entrepreneurship Through Acquisition Practitioner

Reid Tileston

GRIT
IT
DONE

A Low-Risk Guide
to Entrepreneurial
Business Ownership

Published in the United States of America

Paperback ISBN 979-8-9897959-0-1
eBook ISBN 979-8-9897959-1-8

Published by Grit It Done L.L.C.

I would like to dedicate this book to the current and future entrepreneurial business owners (EBOs) throughout the world. You are making the world a better place.

CONTENTS

Disclaimer

I have recreated certain events, people, and conversations from my memories. In order to maintain their anonymity, I have, in most instances, changed the names of individuals, as well as some identifying characteristics and details.

FOREWORD

BY SALLY EDWARDS

There are major themes in every book. This one is no exception. These themes are critical to a deeper understanding of this book's purpose. If you are thinking about starting or are ready to own an entrepreneurial business, this book serves as the tool and the method to do so successfully. Each of these themes can originate differently. But author, athlete, and entrepreneur Reid Tileston's themes come from real-life business experiences, not some business consultant's textbook.

Having graduated with a master's in business administration after the age of forty, I realized quickly that degrees are best valued when one is in the trenches, doing the dirty and fun work and living by the results of business choices. That's just what you get with *Grit It Done: A Low-Risk Guide to Entrepreneurial Business Ownership*.

The first theme Reid shares is his business experience of buying and growing a fitness franchise. Throughout the book, Reid also shares his strategies and execution using the example of how he did it as well as some of the mistakes he made along the way.

The second theme is reaching the finish line. Reid is an ultra-endurance athlete, and he has competed in some of the hardest races in the world. He always finishes. Not all athletes or Entrepreneurial Business Owners (EBOs) are able to do that. Getting to the finish line is something he knows well—especially if it takes grit. Reid has crossed the finish line of an Ironman 140.6, the famous Escape From Alcatraz no-wetsuit swim in the frigid San Francisco Bay, and other ultraevents. You will learn how he gets over the finish line, whether it's a pretty experience or not.

The third theme is credibility and doing the right and honest thing. Too often in business, personal greed, not divulging the whole truth, lack of trust, and fear interfere with what makes us better humans. As Reid writes, "EBOs make Americans better citizens." Reid does not just believe; rather, he follows the creed that doing business right leads to better outcomes and a stronger nation. That is not always the case in business leadership in today's America. As Reid writes in Chapter 7, "Transparent, honest, and transactional is the Reid Tileston style!"

The fourth theme is Reid's own catchphrase, "grit it done." Reid is a good example of this concept. Athletes experience the starting line, the miles in between, and the finish line. It takes determination, willpower, belief, and much more to grit it done. Reid coaches you every step of the way: answering your questions, linking to additional resources, and challenging you with action items.

If you are an experienced entrepreneur and have already been down this path, there are insights here that are new and fresh. I first met Reid when he opened one of his fitness franchises on the same block as the headquarters of my company, Heart Zones, in Sacramento, California. After five decades of starting, growing, and selling small businesses multiple times over, I know that Reid's formulas work.

If you are considering the EBO path, want to invest in EBOs, or want to sell to an EBO, I would encourage you to read this book and interact with Reid. Being in his orbit will endow you with a grit-it-done attitude. The sky is the limit.

Sally Edwards
Best-selling author, professional triathlete, serial entrepreneur,
CEO and founder of Heart Zones and Fleet Feet
heartzones.com
Sacramento, California

INTRODUCTION

Own things, don't run things. Entrepreneurial success goes beyond merely acquiring or opening a business and then putting your blood, sweat, and tears into it. It comes down to whether you are truly an owner. A business works for the owner, yet often owners work for the business. This can look like an equity employee who does not have control or a controlling owner who is working *in* the business as opposed to *on* it. Too often, this leads to a plethora of effort with limited upside at the end—the American norm. The better alternative is to enjoy the journey by being in the driver's seat and reaping meaningful rewards at the finish line—the American dream.

Ultimately, we all desire to own our destiny. While this is a popular trope in American culture, it is surprisingly rare to see people who truly do it. That is because our professional work lives aren't designed to give us this freedom and control. It takes effort, tenacity, commitment, and grit to break out of the most common professional work models to design a life for yourself that will enable you to reach your goals.

In this book, I will share with you the vision for Entrepreneurial Business Ownership—the only professional pathway that provides this level of freedom and autonomy. Entrepreneurial Business Ownership is a model of Entrepreneurship Through Acquisition (ETA), and in this book, I will share the lessons I've learned through buying, owning, operating, investing in, and selling businesses. The Entrepreneurial Business Owner (EBO) life is not for the faint of heart, but it is the best way I know to achieve your goals.

In 1915, the Swiss built a cable railway (called a funicular) up the side of Mount Niesen, a 7,749-foot peak in the Swiss Alps. This funicular has a maintenance staircase that spans 11,674 stairs—seven times the number of stairs in the Empire State Building. To make matters more challenging, it reaches a maximum incline of 68 percent. After eighty-five years, the Swiss had the brilliant idea to hold a race to see who could complete all the steps the fastest. Today, the annual Niesen-Stairway-Run (or Niesen-Treppenlauf) is known as an intense endurance race. When I learned about the race in spring 2021, I knew immediately: I had to do it.

The race is difficult to get into in normal times. There is a lottery (with a low probability of success) to gain entrance. To make matters worse, it had been canceled the previous year due to the pandemic, and demand was so high that they were not adding to the waitlist. Success was not looking likely.

Never one to be intimidated by a challenge, I started a ten-month campaign of emailing the organizers every Friday night. Week after week, I wrote to a man named Nico about my determination to make it into the race—including a special Christmas Eve plea that all I wanted for Christmas was to be in the 2022 climb. Nico responded to every email I sent, and we developed a fun Friday night penpal relationship.

In March of 2022, Santa Claus came through, and I managed to get into the event. The race was on June 11.

I had two goals for the event: 1) to finish, and 2) to smile on the course. Now that I was in, I needed to train to survive the onslaught.

My regime consisted of running the stairs in my high-rise every week-day morning at 4:00 a.m. and again after returning home at 7:00 p.m. I also organized a Thursday night stair-climbing training group where we pushed each other to new heights in the stairwell. Misery loves company. In an effort to best mimic race conditions, I also made week-end trips to the Manitou Incline in Colorado Springs, which features more than 2,700 steps and 2,000 feet of elevation gain, providing the best US-based training ground for Switzerland.

To be sure, there were setbacks. In the critical weeks leading up to the race, I hurt my back while working with some of my field techni-cians, which led to me walking like John Wayne and forced me to cur-tail my final days of training. Yet setbacks were not going to slow me down; getting to the top of the staircase was my destiny. Success was never in doubt.

When the time came, my dad accompanied me on the trip as a spectator. He was an epic runner in his own right, having once com-pleted a 100-mile race in under twenty-four hours. A truly inspira-tional man among men. We were living the father-son dream. We stayed at a beautiful mountaintop Swiss chalet with a picturesque view of the Jungfrau and Eiger in the background. Watching the sun-set in the Swiss alps was enough to take my breath away despite all my training.

The day of the race, the weather was beautiful. As I picked up my race packet, I heard a voice emphatically yell my name: "Reid!"

Who could that be? I wondered. It was Nico, the man that I had been emailing on Fridays for the past ten months. Nico was in his mid-twenties and sported a smile that was visible from a mile away. We immediately embraced like best friends at a high school reunion. Meeting Nico made me feel at home in a foreign place.

I made my way to the start of the race. The stairwell ahead was a daunting sight. To soothe my nerves, I repeated in my head that conquering this staircase was my date with destiny (thank you, Tony Robbins). The mental game is just as important as the physical one. This was part of my training. I tactically chose happy thoughts in an attempt to be ignorant of the pain and suffering that lay ahead. And when those happy thoughts inevitably slipped to fear of the upcoming pain, I visualized smiling on the stairs. Visualize and you shall realize.

My start time was approaching, so I headed to the funnel of runners that was gathering around the starting line. Start times are staggered, so each runner begins one at a time. I was pumped and ready to race as the line in front of me whittled down. The fun was about to begin. I was hit with a surprise when it was my time to start: the participant immediately in front of me was blind. Let me repeat that: a blind man (with a guide) was racing up the world's tallest staircase. I was awed by his tenacity and felt incredibly honored to be racing with such determined peers.

By step 1,000, the euphoria and excitement had worn off, and I was in pure pain. The road ahead was long and steep. Training on the Manitou Incline and my stairwell had helped, but even that couldn't have fully prepared me for the pain and suffering I was enduring. I chose to smile as my fellow racers cringed, grabbing an epic race photo in the process. The smile did not tell the whole story; the low point of the race came when I was passed by an exceptional athlete who was racing in pink Crocs while I gasped for breath. Nevertheless, I powered forward, overcoming the 68 percent incline, and was rewarded with the pure elation and immense pride (once I caught my breath) when I met my dad and Nico at the top. Mission accomplished.

What made the race even more meaningful was that it marked a life-changing financial and entrepreneurial achievement. In 2019,

I had bought a well run industrial services company, expanded it through the pandemic, made it more profitable, and sold it to a strategic acquirer, generating life-changing wealth.

Running the Niesen-Treppenlauf was how I celebrated my victory. I even put the event date in the company's Purchase Agreement so that there would be no uncertainty.

I got to live my American dream. I closed the deal, made my millions, paid big retention bonuses to all the employees, and got to compete in one of the coolest endurance events in the world. The event kicked my butt in the best kind of way, and yet I was the happiest person on the stairwell. It was an epic father-son endeavor and a great way to celebrate my EBO journey.

I imagine you, too, have plenty of life goals you want to accomplish. Maybe it's to travel the world, retire early, or start a scholarship fund. This book can help you get there.

The Opportunity and Social Good

In the United States, retiring business owners, and especially small business owners, are expected to sell or bequeath $10 trillion in assets over the next twenty years.[1] The cost of unoptimized transitions is significant. According to the Family Business Institute, family-held small businesses, when transitioned from generation to generation, have only a 30 percent chance of lasting into a second generation, 12 percent into a third, and 3 percent into a fourth generation or beyond.[2] Small business acquisition and ownership is a wealth-generating opportunity for EBOs. There are over six million businesses in

---

1 | Lindsey, Kevin, Nathan Mauck, and Ben Olsen. "The Coming Wave of Small Business Succession and the Role of Stakeholder Synergy Theory." *Global Finance Journal* 48 (May 2021): 100457. https://doi.org/10.1016/j.gfj.2018.11.003.

2 | Fernández-Aráoz, Claudio, Iqbal, Sonny and Ritter, Jörg. *Leadership Lessons from Great Family Businesses.* n.d.

the US with at least one employee and approximately ten million that employ at least one non-employee contractor that are target businesses to be purchased from the current owner.[3][4] There are also hundreds of viable de novo franchising opportunities for prospective EBOs to pursue. The upside can be financially rewarding. Let's take an example.

If you buy a business:

- that is generating $500,000 of EBITDA (earnings before interest, taxes, depreciation, and amortization; i.e., cash flow) per year
- at a purchase price multiple of 5x EBITDA
- using 80 percent debt at a 10.5 percent interest rate
- using 20 percent of your own money down
- And if you then:
- grow EBITDA at 5 percent per year
- ensure capital expenditures (capex) are 5 percent of EBITDA
- sell for 5x EBITDA after ten years

On the following page is what the next ten years of your life could look like.

IRR (internal rate of return) is a metric used in financial analysis to estimate the profitability of potential investments, with a 30 percent IRR being an excellent return.

Contrast this with the start-up and hustle culture that permeates today. Data from the BLS (Bureau of Labor Statistics) shows that approximately 25 percent of new businesses make it to fifteen years or more, while around 20 percent of new businesses fail during the first

3 | "Frequently Asked Questions About Small Businesses," US Small Business Administration, March 2023, advocacy.sba.gov/wp-content/uploads/2023/03/Frequently-Asked-Questions-About-Small-Business-March-2023-508c.pdf.

4 | fedsmallbusiness.org/survey/2018/report-on-nonemployer-firms#:~:text=In%20this%20 report%2C%20we%20define,of%20nonemployers%20employ%20contract%20workers.

Year	0	1	2	3	4	5
EBITDA		$500,000	$525,000	$551,250	$578,813	$607,753
Debt Interest		$210,000	$197,136	$182,921	$167,214	$149,857
CapEx		$25,000	$26,250	$27,563	$28,941	$30,388
Purchase Price Depreciation Tax Shield		$66,667	$66,667	$66,667	$66,667	$66,667
After Tax Debt Principal		$122,515	$135,379	$149,593	$165,301	$182,657
Exit						
Owner Pre-Tax Cash Flow	-$500,000	$209,152	$232,902	$257,840	$284,024	$311,517

Year	6	7	8	9	10
EBITDA	$638,141	$670,048	$703,550	$738,728	$775,664
Debt Interest	$130,678	$109,485	$86,067	$60,190	$31,596
CapEx	$31,907	$33,502	$35,178	$36,936	$38,783
Purchase Price Depreciation Tax Shield	$66,667	$66,667	$66,667	$66,667	$400,000
After Tax Debt Principal	$201,836	$223,029	$246,447	$272,324	$300,918
Exit					$3,878,321
Owner Pre-Tax Cash Flow	$340,386	$370,697	$402,525	$435,943	$4,682,686
IRR					55.48%
Return Multiple					14.06

two years of being open, 45 percent during the first five years, and 65 percent during the first ten years. These trends have remained relatively consistent for the last forty years.[5] Certain business owners (the unincorporated self-employed, mostly running things like hairdressers, restaurants, corner shops, etc.) earn 16.5 percent less than the salaried job that they left to be business owners[6] and often run their businesses in such a way that leaves low to no payouts at the end.[7] [8] It is easier to take a proven concept and build it into something that works for you than to constantly hustle forward, scrape by, and accept a limited (or even non-existent) payout at the end.

What Makes an Entrepreneur?

The terms around entrepreneurship are evolving. While entrepreneurship was once associated with Silicon Valley start-ups, the concept has recently transcended disciplines, professions, and societal roles. To help us all get on the same page, here are my definitions around entrepreneurship.

> **Entrepreneur:** *An individual who acts.*

> **Entrepreneurship:** *Minimizing risk while maximizing value in the act of creating.*

5 | "Table 7: Survival of private sector establishments by opening year," US Bureau of Labor Statistics, October 2023, bls.gov/bdm/us_age_naics_00_table7.txt.

6 | Ross Levine and Yona Rubinstein, "Smart and Illicit: Who Becomes an Entrepreneur and Do They Earn More?"2005, Archived by archive.org: web.archive.org/web/20160222033032/http:// faculty.haas.berkeley.edu/ross_levine/Papers/smart_and_illicit_24sep2015.pdf

7 | Adam Debussy, "BizBuySell Insight Report," BizBuySell, October 2023, bizbuysell.com/ insight-report

8 | Mary Ellen Biery, "Studies Show Why Many Business Owners Can't Sell When They Want To,"Forbes.com, February 5, 2017, forbes.com/sites/sageworks/2017/02/05/ these-8-stats-show-why-many-business-owners-cant-sell-when-they-want-to/?sh=4f0fa01744bd

Entrepreneurial mindset: *Being resilient, resourceful, and solution-oriented.*[9]

With these definitions under our belt, let's talk about you.

Who Are You?

There are four professional pathways.

Employee

We all know what an employee is: the backbone of a business. Employees solve problems, deal with customers, crunch the numbers, and get things done. The good ones get promoted and grow; the average stay stagnant, and the low performers tend to scurry to the door. As an employee, you don't typically see a direct financial upside for the value that you add. If you do, it can get mired in organizational politics. Employees do not own all of the upside of their work. Job security is not guaranteed and is often dictated by forces outside an employee's control.

Equity Employee

An equity employee's job is to make investors money. A CEO is an example of an equity employee. They get meaningful equity in the company that they run, so they own a portion of their upside. They are not the controlling owner. They do not own the majority of the upside of their work, nor do they have control over the company. Their job security depends on the wishes of the board. Even owner-CEOs who acquire a business through a search fund—a pool of capital funded by

9 | Meredith Somers, "3 traits of an entrepreneurial mindset," MIT Management Sloan School, November 23, 2022, mitsloan.mit.edu/ideas-made-to-matter/3-traits-entrepreneurial-mindset#:~:text=An%20entrepreneurial%20mindset%20is%20resilient,are%20critical%20thinkers%2C%20Barrett%20said.

investors—are beholden to those investors and have limited power in decision-making.

Business Owner

Business owners own their upside—that is, they take home the profits of whatever improvements and efforts they implement. Yet often, the business owns *them* more than they own the business. Business ownership too often becomes a dead-end job that pays the bills while leaving calendar control and financial freedom on the table. Businesses like this have limited resale value. Business owners often trade the security of employment with good benefits—which lacks autonomy—for self-employment, which has autonomy yet lacks the benefits. I love business owners and have spent many years as one. I hope that this book will inspire many of these business owners to dream bigger and step forward into entrepreneurial business ownership.

Entrepreneurial Business Owner (EBO)

An EBO is living the dream. They own their upside, control their calendar, and experience true autonomy. They apply the entrepreneurial mindset to business ownership and have the systems in place so that the business can operate without them. When they choose to work on the business, they do the blocking and tackling when it comes to creating equity value. An effective EBO owns their business and in doing so owns their life. This book will teach you how to be an EBO. But becoming an EBO does not have to happen overnight. In fact, a great path to being an EBO is to first use a traditional ETA Search Fund to acquire a business and become the CEO, learn the tricks of the trade, make some money, and then use that money to buy your own business or a franchise and be an EBO.

Here is a chart to help you understand where you are on the spectrum, and how you might be able to level up different aspects of your professional life through the lessons in this book.

	Do you have a boss?	Is your job at the peril of a board or boss?	Do you own the majority of your upside?	Do you control your company?	Do you spend the majority of your time engaging in activities that create equity in your business?
Employee	YES	YES	NO	NO	NO
Equity Employee	YES	YES	NO	NO	YES
Business Owner	NO	NO	YES	YES	NO
Entrepreneurial Business Owner	NO	NO	YES	YES	YES

Who Am I?

I have been all four at points in my career.

April 2007:

I was an employee. I quit my job in finance in San Francisco with $100,000 in the bank to open Anytime Fitness clubs.

December 2007:

First fitness club opens.

2007-2022:

For my first club, I was an equity employee; for my second club, I was a business owner; for my third club, I became an EBO. I was a top-performing Anytime Fitness multi-unit owner and EBO investor.

2013-2015:

MBA from the University of Chicago Booth School of Business where I ran the ETA Club, helped plan the first ETA Conference, and was the teaching assistant for the first ETA class where I helped design the curriculum.

2016-2019:

Investing and searching for another business to buy and run with a mix of corporate jobs.

2019-2022:

Bought, grew, and sold an industrial services business.

2024:

Teach ETA at Case Western Reserve University, investing, board member, coaching, doctoral-level ETA research, writing and speaking. Exciting times ahead!

The Power of Entrepreneurial Business Ownership

Most Americans want autonomy, calendar control, impact, and the ability to own the upside of their work that's typically thought to come with small business ownership.

America believes in small businesses. A June 2023 Gallup poll found that 65 percent of Americans have a "great deal" or "quite a lot" of confidence in small business, compared with 14 percent who have confidence in big business and only 8 percent who have confidence in Congress.[10] Why are we so confident in small businesses? Twenty-nine percent of this confidence is derived from the perception that small businesses represent the American Dream and are the backbone of the economy, and another 28 percent comes from the business owner's ability to be personally invested in the company.[11] In fact, Americans are 6 percent more confident in small business than they are in science.[12]

10 | https://news.gallup.com/poll/1597/confidence-institutions.aspx

11 | https://news.gallup.com/opinion/polling-matters/216674/business-gets-bigger-even-americans-prefer-small.aspx

12 | https://news.gallup.com/poll/1597/confidence-institutions.aspx

Not only that, but entrepreneurial business ownership is good for society. The country needs more EBOs. A few points worth reviewing:

- **The Job Creators:** According to the Small Business Administration (SBA), small businesses (fewer than 500 employees) generated 12.9 million net new jobs between 1995 and Q2 2021, meaning small businesses have accounted for 66 percent of employment growth over the last twenty-six years.

- **Economic Engine:** 43.5 percent of economic activity (Gross Domestic Product) is attributed to small businesses.[13]

- **The Breeding Ground:** Small businesses grow. Household names such as Nike, Under Armour, and Ben & Jerry's started off as small businesses.

- **Innovation:** The smallest research and design businesses engage in the most patenting activity per employee, and some of the greatest innovations in US history have come from small businesses. Microsoft, Facebook, and Google are prime examples of how small business innovations can change the world.[14]

- **Ecosystem:** Businesses that grow often remain in the community in which the business started, creating an ecosystem for further entrepreneurship while supporting other small businesses. As an example, look at what Salesforce has done in San Francisco.

- **Local Community Support:** When consumers patronize local small businesses, they are giving money back to their local community. For every dollar spent at a local business, $0.67

13 | cdn.advocacy.sba.gov/wp-content/uploads/2018/12/21060437/Small-Business-GDP-1998-2014.pdf

14 | cdn.advocacy.sba.gov/wp-content/uploads/2022/09/13092425/Fact-Sheet_Small-Business-Innovation-Measured-by-Patenting-Activity.pdf?utm_medium=email&utm_source=govdelivery

stays in the local community, with $0.44 as wages and $0.23 invested in other local businesses.[15]

- **Sheer Numbers:** 99.9 percent of all businesses with at least one employee are small businesses, and small businesses employ 61 million Americans, 46.4 percent of the US workforce.[16]

With all these benefits, it's easy to see why people choose to become business owners; however, as mentioned earlier, starting and operating a small business often doesn't provide the freedom owners are hoping for. The best way to serve society *and* accomplish your own dreams is entrepreneurial business ownership.

That said, the road to being an EBO is risky. The competition is always on your heels, team members are a challenge to handle, and financing is rarely fun. Failure can have high costs, including bankruptcy and frayed personal relationships. Success is far from guaranteed, and at times even hard work is not enough.

This book provides a method for reaping the promised rewards of being an EBO while minimizing your financial, personal, and professional risks. It provides autonomy, the ability to have an impact, and a test of self-efficacy for those willing to take on the challenge. When executed well, entrepreneurial business ownership can create generational wealth.

Being an EBO is stimulating. The ecstasy, elation, and excitement of being all-in is amazing. Take a step back, inhale deeply, close your eyes, and envision a life with a clear professional purpose. The clear purpose is your business and the people whose lives you will enhance along the way—especially your own. This is what I discovered

---

15 | roseville.ca.us/news/what_s_happening_test/shop_roseville_s_small_businesses_

16 | cdn.advocacy.sba.gov/wp-content/uploads/2021/12/06095731/Small-Business-FAQ-Revised-December-2021.pdf

firsthand in my twenties and have been able to replicate with multiple other companies. Entrepreneurial business ownership has given me a reliable, fun way to make excellent money and become more civic minded. I am now an EBO enthusiast.

I am excited for you to embark on this journey. I believe that with the insights from this book, we can minimize the risk of business ownership and provide a road map to make entrepreneurial business ownership accessible to swaths of Americans. There are excellent opportunities to acquire an existing business, franchise, or license that provides the freedom, autonomy, security, self-expression, and wealth generation opportunities of entrepreneurial business ownership.

My Journey to Entrepreneurial Business Ownership

I started as an unpaid intern at a start-up finance firm in San Francisco with a desire to level up my career. I had no idea how to do it—but that all changed in one happy hour with two private equity professionals at the second oldest bar in San Francisco. I was plotting the next steps in my career. Do I stay in finance? Move to China to gain fluency in Chinese? Start a company? Or …?

These private equity pros were looking at acquiring a franchisor in Minneapolis called Anytime Fitness. While the deal ultimately did not close, they learned that franchise locations were low-cost and high-profit. They pitched me on the idea, and I was off to the races.

I had flipped my unpaid internship into a paid job in a trendsetting secondary venture capital/private equity firm, and I was making respectable money. By April 2007, I had $100,000 in cash.

Let's explore what could have happened if I had stayed on the traditional course. We can make a few assumptions: compensation earnings potential of $100,000 per year in 2007, with an increase of 10 percent per year, 30 percent after-tax savings rate, and 10 percent annual return on savings. While there is plenty of room for debate on these numbers, they represent a fair starting point. After sixteen years, with inflation, that $100,000 would be worth $143,729. If invested in the S&P 500, it would be worth $273,600. By May 2022, I would have an after-tax net worth of approximately $1.5 million. Not bad.

But life is all about alternatives, and I'm glad I took a chance on entrepreneurial business ownership. What did all this get me? After sixteen years of being a business owner in fitness, industrial services, environmental compliance, and investing, my net worth is significantly higher.

This Book Can Be the First Step for You

The purpose of this book is to empower the EBO-in-waiting to take step-by-step intentional action toward becoming an EBO. There is a tried-and-true method to maximizing your chances of success. Following the steps outlined in this book will make your journey low-risk, relative to your alternatives. Controlling your destiny, purpose, and autonomy awaits.

The method outlined in this book features nine steps spread over nine chapters:

- Chapter 1 is about having an EBO mindset.
- Chapter 2 will help you understand your end-vision and goals for being an EBO, illustrating that if you are not all-in, you are in the way.
- Chapter 3 will provide a framework for understanding how to evaluate an opportunity, illustrating that optionality leads to a better post-close reality.

- Chapter 4 provides a road map for financing—the biggest question every aspiring EBO has before they start. A key point here is that if the opportunity is good, the money will follow.
- Chapter 5 teaches you how to close, illustrating the essential need for grit and perseverance.
- Chapter 6 delves into building a winning team, illustrating that absentee ownership is earned by cultivating entrepreneurial employees.
- Chapter 7 proves the importance of peer groups that can empower you.
- Chapter 8 will provide guidance for how to run your business so that it is always positioned for sale. Work hard now to get rewarded later.
- Finally, Chapter 9 will teach you how to execute a transaction if you desire.

I know entrepreneurial business ownership can feel daunting and risky. This is the book I wish I'd had when I was beginning my journey sixteen years ago. By following the recommendations and advice in each chapter, you'll be able to lower the risk for each step of your journey. When each step is low-risk, the entire journey is low-risk—all while the upside remains. Following these steps will also save you money, time, and mental anguish. I am going to share the best practices I've acquired along the way so that as many individuals as possible can achieve wealth generation through entrepreneurial business ownership and become better people at the same time. Until now, much of the knowledge in this book has been reserved for graduates of top MBA programs, private equity professionals, and business owners. I am thrilled to share what I have learned with you.

Being an EBO will allow you to live your American dream. Kudos to you for making an investment in yourself and your future by picking up this book. Now, let's explore your needs and goals with entrepreneurial business ownership.

CHAPTER 1

THE ENTREPRENEURIAL BUSINESS OWNER MINDSET

Attitude is everything. Most people think that entrepreneurial business ownership is the destination. In reality, entrepreneurial business ownership is a mindset that makes the journey fun.

Mindset matters. The first and last step in being an effective EBO is having a healthy mindset. This chapter is going to review a list of critical dictums that I have learned from other successful practitioners over the years and refined for my own use to get you in the mind of being an EBO. Think of this chapter as a primer before we delve into the details in later chapters. Enjoy!

Good, Better, Best

Once an American behemoth, Sears had three product categories made famous by their catalogs: good, better, and best. Successful EBOs tweak this mantra: *good, better, best, never ever rest until good is better and better is best.* My first fitness club made a few thousand dollars per month; my second was a top 10 percent performer, and my third was a top 1 percent performer. All three businesses ran themselves. Continuous learning, networking, and hiring entrepreneurial employees were key.

The IRR Rule

Internal Rate of Return (IRR) is a metric used in financial analysis to estimate the profitability of potential investments. Professional private equity investors chase investments that have an IRR of at least 30 percent. As an EBO, you should do the same. Hold yourself to the same standard that esteemed investors do.

IRR is calculated using a cash flow analysis. For example, if you invest $500,000 of cash to buy a business, and it generates $125,000 of profits each year for the next four years, along with an additional $750,000 in year four (for $875,000 in total) because the business was sold, then the IRR is 33 percent.

Year	0	1	2	3	4
Cash Flow	-$500,000	$125,000	$125,000	$125,000	$875,000
IRR					33%

Achieving a 30 percent+ IRR requires a combination of buying the business at a fair price, mixing debt and equity, and adding value to the business as an operator. Chasing opportunities that can credibly achieve a 30 percent IRR will allow you to raise money by instilling in you the discipline of a professional private equity investor. Applying the rule will allow you to accelerate your own financial returns. Visit www.reidtileston.com/grititdone for an IRR calculator.

Leave It Better Than You Found It

Your goal as a business owner is to leave your business and your people better than you found them. I owned a business with a fleet of service trucks that were shared among technicians. Every day, the last technician who used the truck was tasked with leaving it in better shape than it was in when they got into it. I felt the same way about the team members: it was my goal to improve their lives in some way while they worked at the company I owned. Whether I was helping them to get a driver's license, attain a certification, file unpaid tax returns, or take on new responsibility, I found no higher calling than improving lives. The same way of thinking applies to your future business. During the research phase, you must understand how you, as the new owner, are uniquely positioned to leave your future business better than you found it.

Grit It Done

There are two kinds of individuals: those who grit it done, and those who find excuses. EBOs grit it done. To me, gritting it done is about doing exactly what you do not want to do precisely when you do not want to do it. Sound fun? It really is (I swear); elation always awaits when the hard stuff is finished. Below is the Grit It Done framework. Take a quick look. We will explore it in greater detail later.

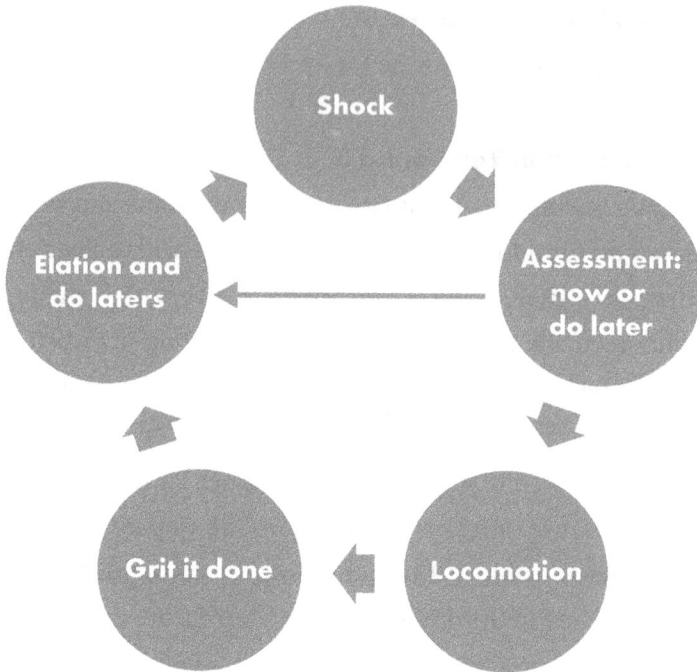

Money Talks

As an EBO, you need to pay to play. Business doesn't happen on good faith agreements alone; you need the cash to back it up. For example, it is critical to be credible and dedicated to doing the deal throughout the courtship and closing process so that others have confidence that you will close the deal. The world is binary; either you close on your opportunity or you don't.

No matter how close you get, the deal is not done until the money is in the bank. For one business I bought, I was diligent in my preparation. The equity check from the bank was in my possession to give to Frank (the seller). The bank was set up to wire the rest. I confirmed with my banker on Wednesday that all was set, and on Thursday, I confirmed that the wire had been sent by the cut-off time. I was confident execution would occur without a hitch. Frank grew nervous as the hours went by. At day's end, we had his bank's treasury office on the line confirming that no money had been received, contrasted with a SWIFT code from my bank confirming that the money had been sent. Lost in cyberspace! It felt like a love story gone wrong. We are both divorced, and Frank's divorce was particularly nasty. I joked that his ex-wife must have hijacked the transfer. Frank did not find this funny. Frank confirmed with his lawyer and was crystal clear that there would be no closing until the money was in the bank. He refused to cash the equity check until the remaining money was there. Actions speak louder than words. While Frank said he was confident the money would come through, we were in limbo until it did. He was stressed, anxious, and unhappy. We left for the evening in limbo with the deal not closed. The celebration had to wait until the next day when the money finally arrived.

The Importance of Power Habits

Atomic Habits by James Clear is a fabulous book outlining the importance of habits and how to cultivate good ones. We are creatures of habit, and my operating philosophy is simple. I seek to maximize good habits and minimize bad ones. When the going gets tough, subconscious habits keep us going and play an important role for successful EBOs. An EBO I know was committed to creating a set number of opportunity leads every weekday, no matter what. Whether sick, traveling, at the finish line of closing on an opportunity, or dealing with family issues, it became a habit that got done.

I believe in the power of habits. While operating the industrial services business every weekday, I got up and ran to the top of my high-rise—seventy-seven flights of stairs and around 400 feet of elevation—followed by a cold shower for approximately two minutes. For me, there is no better way to start the day. At the end of the day, without fail, I repeated this workout in my work clothes, this time followed by a hot shower as a reward. I apply this principle to my personal time and diet as well. On Tuesday nights, I teach my family Chinese; on Wednesdays, I talk to my dad; on Thursdays, I talk to my mom; and on Fridays, I talk to my good friend Simon.

I used power habits to help me stay on top of the seemingly endless to-do list for the company. On weeknights after dinner and before going to bed, I would scrutinize the invoices sent out from the day, along with the schedule for the next day. I would then set out an agenda for the office manager, which we would review to start the day at 8:00 a.m. I was always up at 4:45 a.m., prepared for whatever excitement would start the day.

To be an effective EBO, discipline matters. Key team members would check with me each day to make sure that the schedule was set for the following day. They know how much I love to pay attention to detail and, as time went on, they knew what to expect during our check-outs.

Clarify in Writing

Two successful tech CEOs I know write as their primary form of communication to their team. Their verbal communication skills are excellent, yet they prefer writing. Kurt, my attorney, does almost all his communication via email. I love it. I am a professional paid public speaker, a proponent of the power of spoken words and gestures to educate and inspire. Yet when it comes to transactionally communicating, I always use email and text. Written words are concrete. Having to recollect what was said, discussed, or promised is irrelevant. It is all written. Writing things down forces individuals to organize their thoughts and optimize time.

When I was selling a fitness club, I had a team member on the ground to give club tours to prospective buyers. I also did not use an intermediary to list or sell the club. One hundred percent of the communication between the buyer and me was via email, including the deal points and emotional sale items. It was a very efficient transaction. The club's performance and supporting documents spoke for themselves. I could loop others into email chains as needed. Miscommunication did not occur. I discovered any color that needed to be added could happen via email.

Businesses often overestimate the value of meetings. In many cases, we all have better things to do with our time, such as activities that help grow the business, or, in my case, exercising or rejuvenating outdoors. Selling the business via email was a liberating experience. I was free from the burden of scheduling. Once the correspondence started, I took it as a challenge to sell a business without ever talking to the buyer. Mission accomplished! I am transparent and live my life as though every action I take will be scrutinized and publicly available: the good, bad, embarrassing, and euphoric. Writing is powerful because it gives people nowhere to hide. Effective EBOs know how to write more with fewer words, utilize email for accountability, and take advantage of time efficiency.

Keep It Simple

Great EBOs strive to keep it simple. Remember the old saying, *Keep it simple, stupid*? Make it so simple that you could explain it to your pet. The cost is not only money, but time. Time is the ultimate commodity.

Failure Builds Success

Abraham Lincoln suffered a multitude of failures and setbacks, although he did not let them get in his way. He was a transformational and impactful leader who altered the course of history. His experience illustrates that failure is a building block of success. Take a look at a brief timeline from his life:

- Mother died when he was nine in 1818
- Defeated for state legislature in 1832
- Failed in business in 1833
- Elected to state legislature in 1834
- Sweetheart died in 1835
- Defeated for Speaker in 1838
- Defeated for nomination for Congress in 1843
- Elected to Congress in 1846
- Lost renomination in 1848
- Rejected for land officer in 1849
- Defeated for US Senate in 1854
- Again, defeated for US Senate in 1858
- Elected president in 1860
- Untimely death of youngest son at age 11 in 1862

As an EBO, you will encounter setbacks big and small, and how you respond to them will define you. Be like Lincoln: treat failure as a building block for success.

Be Uncompromising When It Matters

Business owners get frustrated when things are not done properly. EBOs are uncompromising in their efforts to get things right. At the industrial services business, in 2019 there was a long-standing tough maintenance job that needed to be done late on Friday afternoons, but technicians consistently shortcut the job to get home to their families and start their weekends. As EBOs and leaders, we can make one of two choices: 1) tolerate mediocrity; or 2) get out there and set a high standard. Our response as a company was to get leaders in the field, staying late on a Friday to lead by example and show how the job needed to be done. The results of this effort are that we retained a long-time customer and in the process reinforced our grit-it-done culture.

The Golden Rule: Those Who Have the Gold Make the Rules

The party that controls the scarce resource makes the rules. Kate was an employee whose job I could do myself or hire for, but she was resisting the changes to the business. My line of thinking was, *If she gets in line—great. If she gets fired—great.* Hard power wins out. I was not going to let Kate inhibit our transition from on-premise technology to the cloud, so I recruited a replacement for her that I was excited about. I had the gold; I made the rules.

Financing offers a clear illustration of the Golden Rule. When you take on bank financing, you are submitting to the covenants, rules, and restrictions of the loan. On the other hand, taking on majority outside equity means operators are giving up control of the business and upside. Be thoughtful about your sources of capital, as they have the gold and will make the rules.

What Gets Focus Gets Done

It is easy to get distracted in today's world. We often end up taking on a variety of projects to a mediocre end. Effective EBOs focus on the metrics that matter and allocate resources that will drive success. The customer repeat rate was a critical component for my leisure consumer services business. As the saying goes, *It is cheaper to keep a customer than acquire a new one.* With disciplined focus on the customer repeat rate, I was able to drive results and increase the value of the business. While other metrics suffered, improvement on the metric that mattered most provided the highest upside.

No Time Like the Present

Failure to move fast can be costly. Do not put off till tomorrow what you can do today. For example, I owned a business that fielded emergency calls such as cleaning up overflowing grease traps. As an EBO, I quickly learned that moving fast during emergencies was critical. If we got a customer off the hook when they needed us, they would often reward us with lucrative, long-term, recurring service contracts with minimal consideration for price.

With these essential principles of the EBO mindset under our belt, we are going to dive into the details of how to become an EBO. Next up on the docket is the importance of being all-in. After all, if we are halfway in, we are halfway out.

Action Item

Visit www.reidtileston.com/grititdone and vote for your favorite dictum from the list above.

CHAPTER 2

ASSESSING YOUR READINESS

If you are not all-in, you are in the way. Most people think that being all-in is risky. In reality, it is a great way to de-risk.

As an EBO, you must be all-in. I learned the importance of being all-in when I took up no-wetsuit swimming at the mighty South End Rowing Club, a truly spectacular place in San Francisco full of kindred adventure seekers. The temperature in the San Francisco Bay varies from the high forties to the low sixties. Getting into the water is painful. Many swimmers take their time, slowly easing into the water to acclimate their bodies.

I take a different approach. With a gregarious grin, I fully immerse myself as fast as I can. This challenge was amplified when I swam bareskinned in Lake Michigan in Chicago through winter, where the water and air temperature combined rarely hit fifty. I prefer to lean into the sharp pain of the cold water, knowing that the elation, as my body adapts to the water, is mere minutes away. I go all-in!

When Michael Dayton, founder and CEO of a manufacturing company, said, "If I am not all-in, I am in the way," at our Entrepreneurs Organization (EO) Forum, the words hit me with the force of a Mack Truck. EO is a group of small business owners. We had all wrestled with commitment (or lack thereof) from employees, vendors, and, at times, ourselves. Michael reminded us of a universal truth: the absence of commitment is a killer. A small business CEO once told me, "The key to being a successful business owner is to work a half day every day. The question is: which half?" I resonate with the gem, *The harder I work, the luckier I seem to get.*

An unrivaled level of commitment is a necessary part of the entrepreneurial business ownership equation. There are precious few things that we control in life, but the ability to be all-in is one. Coupling an all-in attitude with strategically aligning potential business opportunities to your background and aspirations is key.

Align to Your Background and Aspirations

Once you have decided that you are all-in, the next step is strategic alignment. I was recently mentoring an aspiring EBO named John. John had a varied professional background, including financial services. He had a lifelong passion for managing money, and his heart clearly desired to be in that industry. I counseled John to align his search for a business to this industry—one he already knew and was passionate about. By focusing on financial services, his knowledge, network, and prospect of opportunities will grow, and his career will be better off whether or not he finds the right company to buy.

When I conducted my own search for a second business to buy, I focused on fitness and franchising. If I did not find a business to purchase, I would still be able to find a good job or opportunity in either of those industries. Like John, win or lose, I would be better off.

Understanding your personal niche is critical to making this a low-risk endeavor. What business are you destined to own and run? Your personal niche can be anything. For example, Marcus is a current CEO, prospective EBO, and a veteran who helped topple Saddam Hussein. He is looking at buying a niche defense business that qualifies as a veteran-owned small business. Marcus knows a lot about these businesses from his time serving and understands the industry. Sign me up to invest.

Align your business ownership journey to either your background or aspirations—ideally both. This will push your career and life forward independent of the outcome. You are uniquely positioned to understand how to make the journey low-risk or completely risk-free for your life. Ask yourself these questions:

- What industry am I an expert in?
- What area do I aspire to have a career in?
- What business am I destined to run?

Then, like John and Marcus, align accordingly. By aligning your efforts to your goals and/or leveraging your past experiences, the fruits of your focus will pay dividends.

Choose Your Location

The ability to go anywhere is one of the greatest entrepreneurial opportunities. Self Esteem Brands is a lifestyle franchising platform with over 5,000 locations and four million members in thirty-nine countries. They are spread across every continent, including Antarctica. Their first concept, Anytime Fitness, which launched in 2002, thrived as a boutique fitness center in markets with little to no competition.

If you think this sounds too good to be true, think again. In a town of 5,000 people, with a $250,000 investment (most of which can be financed), franchisees are usually able to generate $10,000 plus per month in after-debt servicing cash flow before the doors even open. While these opportunities are all but extinct in the US, and the brand has evolved to new heights through operational innovations, this play-book proved to be a wealth-generating event for hundreds (if not thousands) of franchisees, including me. The catch is that unless you are lucky enough to already live in this kind of town, geographic flexibility is required to pursue the opportunity. When I made the choice to leave finance in San Francisco in 2007 to open my Anytime Fitness clubs, it was with the understanding that I was willing to go anywhere to open and operate the clubs. This flexibility led me on an adventure in the California Central Valley during the heart of the Great Recession, as well as to the beautiful Midwest during the COVID-19 years, and to many other places in between. The monetary rewards were handsome. Geographic flexibility is a benefit.

Go All-In

It is fun to live without limits and have the mandate to do anything. Simon (the broker) and Frank (the seller) could never fully understand why the fitness kid from California wanted to buy an industrial services business. I wanted to buy it because it fit my purchase criteria, which will be discussed in Chapter 3. On paper, I had no business getting into this industry. I was not mechanically inclined and did not like trucks. What I did have was a willingness to get my hands dirty and do anything to be successful, coupled with a fundamentally strong business. It is enjoyable to be all-in.

Armed with the reputation that you know where you want to go and are willing to do anything, intermediaries, sources of capital, and business owners will start to take you seriously. The business owner ecosystem sees a lot of demand, and it is unlikely that everyone who aspires to go down this path will succeed. Players in the business owner ecosystem will not invest time in you or take you seriously if you fail to signal that you are all-in. While an all-in attitude will not solve all of your problems, it is a necessary factor in differentiating yourself from the rest of the crowd.

Flip a Naysayer Into a Supporter

Being all-in will allow you to flip naysayers to supporters. For example, take my first interaction with Tom, a key team member of a company I was looking at acquiring.

Since joining the company in 1987, Tom had clocked so many productive hours that, to save on overtime costs, the owners created the salaried position of operations manager. In that position, Tom put in even more hours, which soon led to a promotion to general manager. He'd been the general manager ever since. Tom was all-in. He had a company car, company-provided phone, and company-provided benefits. His son Taylor had also worked at the company for the last ten years, and his wife was employed by one of the top ten customers. Tom half-joked that the business was his fourth child.

I had become an expert on Tom while doing my due diligence on the business (doing diligence refers to a systematic way to analyze and mitigate risk when researching a business opportunity). I knew his address and credit history and had memorized the details of his performance reviews from the last decade. After my conversation with Tom, I had two days to decide whether to go forward on my acquisition, which had consumed the last two and a half years of my life and, more importantly, would consume my future.

Frank had told Tom that he was going to introduce the new owner to him the next day. Frank was methodical and liked to be in control, but the chicken was out of the coop, and his cash machine was now exposed to risk because his key team members knew about the sale.

I had a lot on the line as well. My entire net worth was going into the deal; I was signing two personal guarantees, and I planned to dedicate all my time and effort to the business. But I am an Eagle Scout, and I live by the motto, *Be prepared.* I was positive about my preparation and, therefore, not worried. I was elated, armored by the fact that I was all-in. An exciting day awaited.

Frank met me in the parking lot. His demeanor was anxious but warm. He was now less anxious about me as a buyer and more excited to get the deal done. I had been working hard to make Frank and Simon, the broker, overcome their doubt that I was the right fit to run this company. I combatted this with charisma; I was resolute in my resolve to push the deal across the finish line. Today was just another day in my unwavering journey.

I had developed a good relationship with Simon. I had asked his advice, and he'd coached me to emphasize business as usual. We entered through the side door, and I waited for Tom to arrive. The force of nature that is Tom Williams was about to be unleashed on me.

I met him at the door, shook his hand, and said, "It is an absolute pleasure to finally meet you and put a face to the name."

I said this with the confidence of someone who had spent many hours researching every aspect of this man's life. I returned to my desk, and he remained standing, leaning against a desk with his arms crossed. Despite the abundance of preparation I'd done, it had not dawned on me until this moment that at six foot five, Tom was taller than me. At six foot three, I usually enjoy a height advantage; I get thrown when this is taken away. The height difference, coupled with the fact that I was seated, meant that a detrimental first impression power dynamic was at play. For a split second, I debated whether it made sense to ask him to take a seat. Instead, I opted to play the hand I was dealt. Let the games begin.

Tom was ready to rumble, and he came out swinging,

"What have you done with your life?" he demanded.

I was shocked. His obvious resentment hit me hard and fast like a sucker punch. My fight response took over. The adrenaline increased. I took a deep breath and reminded myself that Tom's attitude was not a problem because I was armed with the fact that I was all-in. I was putting my entire net worth into the deal, moving across the country, and risking bankruptcy. I was going to work eighty-plus hours per week. Nothing was going to stand in my way.

I said, "Tom, it is not about what I have done in the past; it is what we are going to accomplish here together."

This response temporarily placated him. Powering forward, I took the assumptive close approach and stated, "You and Frank built a great business, and the plan is business as usual for the near future. Tom, you will always have a role at the company."

Being all-in leads to positive emotional contagion, which turns naysayers into supporters. While Tom took what I said with a grain of salt, my thorough follow-up in the months and years ahead cemented the point and led to a fruitful win-win relationship.

Build Credibility

Actions speak louder than words. Talk about being all-in is cheap. Building credibility requires action.

The fourth business I owned was a dirty one, involving cleaning grease traps and factory exhaust systems, among other endeavors. Being able to drive a commercial motor vehicle (CMV) placed you at the top of the pecking order. As an outsider, I was determined to show that I could and would do this work. I viewed getting my CDL (commercial driver's license) as a moral obligation to the business and, frankly, the community (even in 2019, there was a national shortage of truck drivers).

After training with Frank and Adam (a professional trainer) for a few months, I was no longer a hazard to other motorists. It was time to take the test. The exam has three parts: vehicle inspection, back-up, and road. Each test costs $50, pass or fail, and must be completed before moving on to the next. A total of five fails are allowed before a new testing period kicks in. With the CDL shortage in full swing, trainers and testers were in high demand. Since trucks can have Gross Vehicle Weight Ratings (GVWRs) of up to 80,000 pounds and move at high speeds, we all want a competent actor in charge of testing.

I called him Mean Tester Mark. Rapport building with Mark was impossible. He was not your friend. He rarely showed up on time. He was not in a hurry to do anything. He seemed intent on doing the minimum amount of work necessary to complete tasks while taking the maximum amount of time possible. I like people who follow rules and hold individuals accountable, and Mark was good at that. Yet I also like people who celebrate wins, and Mark was never in the mood for that.

I flunked the vehicle inspection and spent the next week watching YouTube videos of my favorite pre-trip tester at a truck driving school in Colorado. I was determined to get my CDL.

During my second attempt, I passed the pre-trip vehicle inspection and, to my and Mark's amazement, the back-up test.

The behind-the-wheel test was next. It was an adventure. Not only did I acquire a number of automatic fails, but my score was so low I had to wait a few weeks before I could retest.

As fate would have it, on my third attempt an ambulance entered the scene as I was making a left turn; I chose to complete the turn and in doing so, automatically failed. Three fails down and two to go.

On attempt number four, I crushed it from the start and managed to pass. I was overcome with excitement. The nightmare had come to an end. True to form, Mark reminded me that I was not a good driver—a true downer until the end. I drove the truck back with a ton of pride.

Getting my CDL taught me that anything is possible, and that what does not kill me only makes me stronger. Despite my repeated failures, my determination to succeed and my diligent studying proved to the rest of my team that I was committed to this business. Slowly, I earned their trust and respect by proving that I was all-in.

As an EBO, you must show grit and determination in the face of setbacks. Tom's hard questions and Mark's high standards would have derailed me without my resolve. When it comes to being an EBO, if you are not all-in, consider yourself in the way.

Make the Transition From Employee to Owner

With the comfort of a nice paycheck and benefits, you may find it tough to make the leap from a W-2 employee to an EBO. I would know: twice, I left the comfort of a six-figure job with excellent benefits, an amazing work life-balance, and a healthy culture (at an investment fund and Microsoft) to buy a company and embark on that journey. Why did I do it? Because working for myself is more enjoyable, and I could make more money. Deals do get done by prospective EBOs who have W-2 jobs. It is just harder and takes longer. According to the Self-Funded Search Study, 46 percent of part-time searchers found a company to buy within a year, compared to 58 percent of full-time searchers.[17] In cases I have observed, people are most likely to be successful where there is a mix of critical factors at play: remote work, access to deal flow, use of interns, and a supportive organization. Take the story of Micky Burns. He works as an associate in private equity where he sources and analyzes deals. Micky identified a compelling mission critical B2B service that was ripe for a roll-up (a roll-up merger is when an investor, such as a private equity firm, buys up companies in the same market and merges them together). A portion of his work was from home or could be done remotely so he could respond to deal issues during business hours. Through a mix of paid time off and scrappy work scheduling, he was able to travel to conduct in-person meetings, which worked magic in building credibility. When he had to go to the office, he was up before work and put in the time after hours to source, line up financing, and talk to prospective investors. His dedication and hard work were enough to convince the seller and investors (me included) that he was all-in.

Another example is Zane Carlisle. Zane had a healthy relationship with his employer, and they came to an agreement that he would work half-time at half-salary for a year while looking for a business to buy, with the understanding that his bosses would be given the right to invest in the company. He bought an excellent internet company that generated outsized returns for his investors.

Alex Zalenski is the inspiration for what is possible. Alex is an EBO who is a student at a top-tier business school. He purchased and operates a plumbing company while still being a full-time student. The company is doing well, and I wish I had invested. Another best practice is using interns to assist with financial modeling, industry research, helping to organize your schedule, and other non-critical

17 |"2023 Self-funded Search Study," Search Invest Group, January 10, 2023, searchinvestgroup.com/study.

blocking and tackling. Good interns will provide tremendous value in exchange for the hands-on experience of seeing how the sausage of searching is made. While it is easier and faster to find a company when you are searching full time, the critical factor is to be able to communicate that you are credible and that you are willing and able to leave or balance your job and other commitments with being an EBO.

Action Item

As you think through starting or continuing an entrepreneurial business ownership endeavor, visit www.reidtileston.com/grititdone to fill out a survey designed to gauge your all-in commitment. Your commitment level will impact the people around you: your team, your family, and the other stakeholders in your life.

CHAPTER 3

SEARCHING FOR THE RIGHT OPPORTUNITIES

Having a number of options when you search will improve your odds of success. People think this journey is about finding a single good company; in reality, it is about finding a number of good opportunities and then thoroughly researching and conducting diligence on them all until one finally closes.

In this chapter, you will learn the process of searching for and researching business opportunities. I learned the most important lesson about finding the right opportunities from my grandmother. At eighteen years old in 1934, she graduated from the University of California, Berkeley with a degree in economics, making her one of the youngest women ever to graduate. She went on to have a highly successful career in economics. Later, when I was in high school and she was semi-retired, she explained basic economics to me over a breakfast of hot chocolate and a California omelet in beautiful La Jolla, California. The laws of economics dictate that supply and demand meet at a price and quantity, which is where commerce happens. If there is no supply, there is no market because there is nothing to buy; if there is no demand, there is no market because there is no one to buy it. This last point is worth repeating. If there is no demand, there is no market. Pursue opportunities where the demand is guaranteed. For example, healthcare is an industry where demand is guaranteed because consumers, in general, will invest to maximize life longevity. By taking your time to understand demand, along with investing in research and doing diligence, you are buying yourself financial freedom.

How to Find a Business

Opportunities to buy businesses are all around you if you know where to look. There are approximately six million businesses with at least one employee in the United States, and there are hundreds of viable franchise licenses waiting to be acquired.

Existing Businesses

Searching for a business to buy can involve working with a third party or conducting a proprietary search. Third parties involve brokers and investment bankers who represent sellers and are paid a fee by the seller when the transaction closes. Of course, because you are buying the business, you are paying the seller, so the fee is paid indirectly by you.

A proprietary search is finding a business that is not for sale and offering to buy it. The benefit of this is that you may be the only potential buyer and may not have to compete with others. The downside is that you will have to do a plethora of work to walk the seller through the process, and because you approached them, there is a higher probability that a deal will fail to close because they have not been prepared for the process by an intermediary. Proprietary sourcing involves utilizing your own network as well as cultivating lists of business owners. It can also be as simple as approaching business owners in your community and asking them about selling.

While searching, time is the most important commodity. Because intermediaries have done a lot of the work for you, they save prospective EBOs time. The pain of proprietary sourcing illustrates the value that intermediaries provide. There are plenty out there. The quality of intermediaries runs the gamut; qualify them, and invest your time with the right ones. Ask questions to make sure you have all the information: How many deals have you closed? How long have you been an intermediary? Ask for references to past clients or vendors, such as lenders, attorneys, or ESCROW agents. I have bought and sold businesses with and without an intermediary.

An intermediary must first convince a seller to explore selling the business with their help. Like buying a business, convincing a seller to have representation is usually time-consuming and challenging. The process for an intermediary to win business can take years, often involves competition, and can be fraught with indecision and change given the fickle nature of some sellers. It is also not uncommon for intermediaries to have a personal relationship with the seller, adding an additional layer to navigate. Having put that much skin in the game, intermediaries are generally hungry to prove themselves to their clients by bringing them good buyers that fit the seller's criteria. As an EBO, your job is to come across as credible to both purchase and operate the business. Having a ready-made personal financial statement or investor letters showing financial wherewithal and a one-pager showing your impressive background is a great start. Effective EBOs will go above and beyond by doing extra credit activities such as getting face time with the intermediaries (I used to drive to seller meetings with the intermediaries), beefing up their one-pager with a video to add flavor, or sending gift baskets. Intermediaries have businesses for sale coming down the pipeline and it is not uncommon for their best opportunities to sell before hitting the open market. You want to be at the top of their mind when the good businesses arrive. Pick a strategy that works for you. One EBO I know told an intermediary that he would pay more cash than any buyer for a certain type of deal and successfully asked to get a first crack to bid on incoming deals, while another sent a message that he would not pay the most, but he would invest in keeping the culture of the business stable. Sellers are people, and different sellers have different utility points at exit. Good intermediaries will work with sellers on what matters to them in the sale and screen buyers. Having a personal brand can work in your favor. The best intermediaries have relationships with credible buyers, including private equity firms, family offices, current EBOs, strategic acquirers, and well-heeled prospective EBOs. Think through why you are the right buyer as you approach intermediaries.

Franchising

Acquiring a franchise is the middle ground between starting a business and buying an existing one. When buying a franchise, you are buying a proven business model. There are approximately 7.9 million franchise establishments in the US, employing 8.5 million people and representing $827 billion of economic activity across a plethora of industries.[18] When looking to start a franchise, you have the option of reaching out to an intermediary, in this case a franchise consultant, or reaching out to a franchisor directly. Franchise requirements vary; some require

18 | https://www.statista.com/topics/5048/franchising-in-the-us/#:~:text=In%202022%2C%20it%20 was%20estimated,totaling%20almost%208.5%20million%20people.

specific industry experience and high amounts of liquid capital ready to invest, while others are low-cost and available to prospects of all professional backgrounds. Keep in mind that franchise consultants are often paid by franchisors out of the initial franchise fees that you pay when acquiring a franchise territory. In certain respects, franchising is akin to buying a business owner job, which can lay the groundwork to becoming an EBO. While the franchisor has to consider brand protection and the opportunity cost of letting you operate in the territory, the franchisor is not sharing in the same downside risk that you are as an owner while taking meaningful upside through the myriad of fees.

Search Plan

There are numerous resources to look for franchise opportunities and businesses for sale. Start with free websites such as entrepreneur.com for their top franchise list and bizbuysell.com for existing businesses. Eventually, consider moving on to paid ones, such as krokit.com for franchising or axial.com for existing businesses. As you develop a nuanced search plan, use trade shows, well-networked industry experts, your own personal network, business owner groups, and even business owner lists, coupled with thoughtful outreach and engagement, to position yourself for success. To position yourself for success you must build credibility with the intermediaries, advisers, and owners that you interact with along the way by being all-in and aligning to your background and aspirations.

Industry

The best industry to target is one you know and understand. I have worked with successful EBOs in landscaping, industrial distribution, FedEx routes, autism clinics, window washing, drain cleaning, food service, and many others. High-growth industries with tailwinds are attractive for obvious reasons. There are also compelling opportunities in low-growth, stagnant, or shrinking industries where a company has a niche. For example, one EBO I know is doing a roll-up of traditional retail shops that are engaged at a rudimentary level in e-commerce where he can bring in his expertise to help improve their profits by optimizing their ad spend while also providing a back-office platform to minimize expenses. I invite you to browse historical SBA loan default rates by industry for a sense of where EBO failures have historically come from and the Inc. 5000 (inc.com) for companies that are experiencing fast growth. When researching industries, IBIS Worldwide (ibisworld.com) publishes data on industry statistics and trends, making it a good resource for EBOs. While there is a steep subscription fee to join IBIS, EBOs can find ways to get access for far below the list price, including by joining searchfunder.com. When viewing industry reports, I encourage you to read both about industries you have experience in and industries that are new to you for perspective on the value of the reports. Industry is only one piece of the puzzle. The framework introduced in the next section provides a holistic tool.

How to Analyze a Business Opportunity: Have a Framework

To help you analyze and assess possible franchise or other acquisition opportunities, I've created a framework I call the Double Diamond. This framework is a helpful guide during the searching phase as you analyze opportunities all the way up until you complete the transaction.

There are four key components to think through when analyzing an opportunity: customers, competitors, suppliers, and team. Each of these components should then be analyzed through four additional metrics: concentration, sustainability, power, and Plan Z.

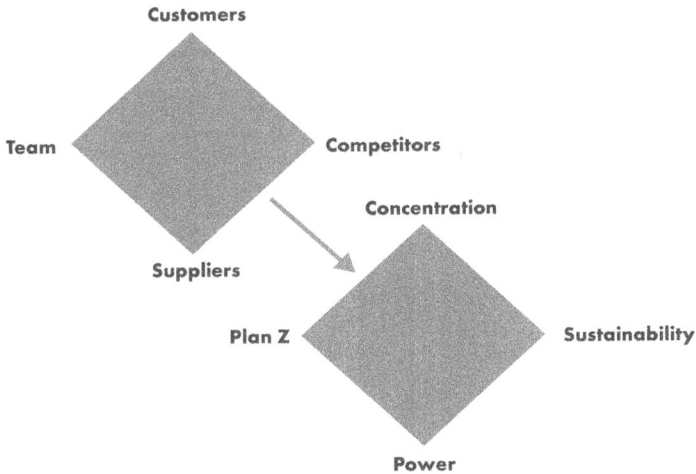

The Double Diamond Framework

Double Diamond Components

Customers: Those who are paying the bills.

Competitors: Those who are doing what the business is doing, as well as those who are a threat to what the business is doing.

Suppliers: Those who provide you with your products and services, such as headsets for a virtual reality company or emergency truck towing for a trucking company.

Team: Your ability to stack the bench with A-players and coaches. Think about your own role in the business.

Double Diamond Metrics

Concentration: Do your top few customers account for a large portion of your revenue and/or profits? What about your suppliers and your team members?

Power: Think about short-term circumstances beyond your control that have the ability to handicap the business, such as the government deciding to stop paying vendors, a key employee leaving, or a social media app changing their algorithm.

Sustainability: Think about long-term risks. How likely are the suppliers to be around in a year? How likely is it that competition will stay away into the foreseeable future? What is the outlook on demand for your industry and service? Think about how things may change.

Plan Z refers to how you will react (what you can control) in case an unforeseeable event happens, such as your top two suppliers burning down in a fire or your entire workforce getting sidelined by a pandemic. An example of Plan Z through the prism of running out of cash would be having access to a line of credit to provide liquidity to weather the storm or having a family member willing to float you money.

The way the Double Diamond works is that you run the components through each metric and assign each metric a score of 0 (bad) through 10 (excellent), add them up, and divide by 40. Assign the corresponding letter grade (A, B, C, D, or F, just like in school) to the percentage, and you have your score. You can visit www.reidtileston.com/grititdone to access the calculator or fill in the sheet below.

After you've calculated the score for each component, calculate the total Double Diamond score.

	Customers	Competitors	Team	Suppliers
Concentration				
Sustainability				
Power				
Plan Z				
Score				
Percentage (divided by 40)				

Add up the score in all of the boxes and enter it here: _____.

Now divide that number by 160: _____ percent.

I will move forward to the next step if the score is 80 percent (128/160) or higher for all components and no less than 60 percent (24/40) for any one component.

Let's see how the Double Diamond works in practice.

I was looking at an industrial services business specializing in a handful of services. One was grease-trap pumping—a service provided to many restaurants and facilities you probably frequent. Grease trapping involves a pumper truck manned by a technician vacuuming out a below-ground tank full of grease. Most jurisdictions mandate that grease traps be cleaned periodically.

Another service this company provides is cleaning food-service kitchen exhaust systems, a service that is required to be performed periodically by the fire department. We fielded our fair share of frantic calls because the owner had neglected to do the work for years and was now faced with an angry inspector who needed the work done yesterday. An ounce of prevention is worth a pound of cure.

Another service we provided was changing air filters and cleaning duct work in factories. Insurance underwriters dictate that a certain number of cleanings are required per year to minimize fire hazards. The customer risks losing their insurance or having a significant premium bump if they skimp on the servicing. As long as food service establishments generate grease and factories continue to generate "gunk" in the air, the business would be in demand.

Disposal sites were key to the grease-trap pumping business, so I arranged a conversation with the main disposal site while doing diligence. I liked the grease-trap pumping service—the biggest and fastest-growing part of the business—most. For the grease-trap pumping business, the disposal research was critical: I needed to assess the sustainability of that operation. The main disposal site was both a customer and a supplier. When they had spills and emergency pumping work needed to be done, this business would quickly bail them out. We were also their go-to for regular maintenance work. It was a happy relationship.

"Will things continue business as usual as both a customer and a vendor?" I asked the plant operator John.

"Yes," John said.

"Do you know of any reason that you guys would stop accepting our grease?" I asked.

"No," he said. "Just keep on providing good service and continue to pick up the phone when we call and need you!"

While the conversation was positive, it was important to think through Plan Z. There were four places where the business was able to dispose of grease, in addition to other business lines to lean on in case of a grease-disposal service interruption. The business was agile. If our main disposal site closed, the business would be able to use the other three while also shifting to other business lines. Another positive factor was that our main disposal site proposed signing a formal service agreement, which was a concrete signal that they desired a stable relationship going forward. There had been short-term service interruptions in the past. I made the base-case assumption that they would happen with similar frequency again in the future and the low-case assumption that the main disposal site would close, there would be problems at the back-up ones and that we may need to significantly curtail the grease business. I also took into account that, in the long run, I could build a disposal site or raise money to purchase the main one. In short, the disposal site risk, while gut-wrenching, was manageable. I felt comfortable with my Plan Z of leaning on the other business lines and using the back-up disposal options, knowing I could scrap to come up with other disposal options if needed.

As is often the case in the world of an EBO, an unwelcome surprise came my way: a few months after purchasing the business, they stopped accepting our grease for a year. The excitement did not stop there. John eventually left his position. They brought on an awesome new operator who had things going in the right direction when, out of left field, the owners decided it was time to close the plant. They were not interested in selling; the real estate was going to be turned into a parking lot. The key takeaway is that while the operator had every intention to continue the relationship, other factors were out of their control.

There were three other options that we leaned on at first. Eventually, one of those backed away completely. I sourced an additional one that we came to rely on. The other two weren't always reliable due to their own operational issues and the inherent pain that grease-trap pumpers cause to disposal sites. Plan Z came to fruition. At one point, none of the four original disposal sites were taking our grease!

Most EBOs have a similar story. Expect the unexpected. The pumping business continued to grow, and we pumped a lot of grease; we just did more non-grease pumping that offered different options for disposal. The fact that the business had multiple revenue streams meant that when the grease disposal got more expensive and became problematic, we could lean on the other business lines. A fragmented customer and supplier base are key.

Here is what the supplier's component looked like when run through the Double Diamond:

Suppliers	
Concentration	8
Sustainability	6
Power	6
Plan Z	9
Score	29
Percentage (divided by 40)	72.5% (C GRADE)

For suppliers, I rated concentration an eight, sustainability a six, power a six and Plan Z a nine. While it was a high-stress time for the business, we were at least partially prepared and able to weather any storms with minimal damage. Notice how 29/40 is a 72.5 percent—which is below my move-forward threshold of 80 percent—but other parts of the business more than compensated. To avoid bias when using the Double Diamond, it is a smart practice to have your peers run the opportunity through it and take the average. I run each opportunity by a minimum of four experienced investors or operators.

The DNA of Strong Demand

Demand drives revenue, which is the starting point for financial freedom. However, not all revenue is created equally. Understanding the importance of cash-friendly revenue, recurring revenue, and high-margin revenue is critical. Revenue that is one-time, low-margin, and hard to collect is less valuable than recurring, cash-friendly, and high-margin revenue. By hitting all three, you position yourself for success.

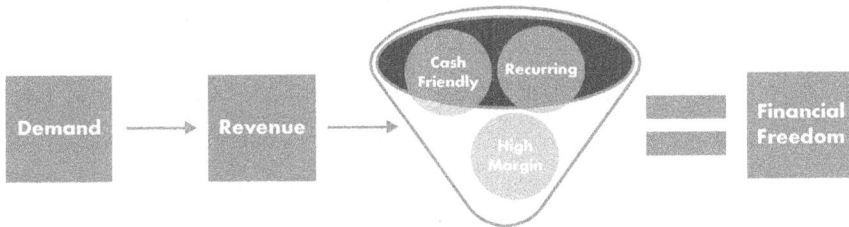

High-Margin Revenue

In-demand businesses can attain high margins. I acquired a business that had a pricing rule worth remembering: all the marginal costs associated with a job (such as labor, fuel, job-specific supplies, etc.) should sum up to 33 percent of the revenue. If it was more than 33 percent, the price of the service should be raised. Put another way, 33 percent cost percentage is equivalent to 67 percent gross profit margins. The business had 45 percent EBITDA margins (a rough estimate of cash flow from operations) when I acquired it. For reference, 20 percent EBITDA margins are considered healthy, making 45 percent amazing. In time, I discovered that some jobs yielded 90 percent-plus gross margins (revenue minus all costs directly associated with the job, but excluding overheads such as rent), while some jobs yielded less than 50 percent gross margins. With knowledge gained before purchasing the business (more on that later) and the customer conversations, I planned to more strictly enforce the 33 percent rule, and for capex (capital expenditure) heavy jobs, I wanted to lower it to 25 percent. Put another way, before purchasing, I knew that gross margins were going to range between 66 and 90 percent. When I eventually sold the business, our overall EBITDA margins were 53 percent. There has been an influx of academic work done on pricing strategy in recent years, which has led to increased pricing optimization in the market. In my case, before closing I talked to the customers about the viability of raising prices to get comfortable.

High margins are important because they provide an operational cushion.

I'm glad I made this a priority before purchasing because later these margins covered me while I learned the business and made mistakes. And as an inexperienced operator in the space, I made my fair share of mistakes that hurt margins. One example was reducing the practice of requiring unpaid lunches for team members. My heart and mind were in the right place. My idea was for our team members to start taking shorter paid breaks and work through lunch, but all that ended up happening was that the lunch breaks were taken out of habit and not logged. So much for the honor system. The team members got a de facto 6.25 percent pay bump, which they did not view as a raise because I had communicated that they were "entitled" to their breaks by law. There was no measurable improvement in productivity or morale. In fact, I probably hurt productivity and morale by the sloppy way I rolled it out, as we developed some trust issues around the logging of meals. With high margins, a mistake like this is digestible. It was a good lesson learned, and I became a better operator because of it. I shy away from low-margin businesses.

When I owned fitness clubs, I also achieved high gross margins. With full-time managers in place, annual gross margins ranged between 35 and 50 percent—$10,000 to $15,000 per month per club in seller discretionary earnings/adjusted EBITDA. In-demand pricing power is key. Strong demand allowed me the flexibility to attain these margins.

Recurring vs. Repeat Revenue

I am presented with a plethora of investment opportunities in the fitness space. The main metric I care about is the membership retention rate. This metric filters through to countless other meaningful operational metrics. A well-run club will have a high retention rate. As two of my professor mentors, Dale and Bill, love to point out, recurring revenue is contractual revenue that requires no additional action on the customer's part to come in. One example is the subscription fee that hotels pay to the specialized companies that provide their wireless internet.

Repeat revenue, on the other hand, requires the customer to proactively place the order. They may have placed the same order hundreds of times before, but action is required to place the order again. Ordering a pizza is an example. A regional pizza chain can predict, with reasonable accuracy, how many pizzas will be ordered on a given day by analyzing historical trends; however, that revenue isn't guaranteed. On the other hand, with recurring revenue, barring a breakdown of the financial system, revenue is coming to the coffers. Fitness revenue is recurring revenue, while an annual factory cleaning that requires a new Purchase Order (PO) each year is repeat revenue. When analyzing businesses, prioritize recurring revenue over repeat revenue.

What's the secret to running a top-performing fitness franchise?

As a reward for making it this far in the book, I am going to give you a real nugget: the secret to being a top-performing fitness franchisee.

Here it is: Automatically deduct the membership dues from a checking or savings account. Let me repeat that. Automatically deduct the dues from a checking or savings account—that is, get an account number and routing number. The fees will be lower than with a debit or credit card, and account numbers change less often than credit card numbers.

For additional bonus points, default to eighteen-month agreements with automatic renewal. I have run the numbers, and the strongest predictor of member retention was whether they were a monthly-recurring-dues member paying from their checking account. There were other meaningful factors too, but this was the most significant. One of my locations consistently had one of the highest retention rates in the system thanks to a combination of culture, ACH payments, and location in an in-demand market. ACH and contractual agreements with automatic renewal are the gold standard of recurring revenue.

For its part, the industrial services business had an amazing run of repeat revenue. In the business marketing materials, they boasted a customer repeat rate of 85 percent. I choose to trust but verify. At my insistence, Simon (the broker) sent me the raw and anonymous QuickBooks data in a massive file. Such efforts and access can make buying through an intermediary worthwhile. I wanted to know if they were blowing smoke with that number.

They were indeed! The actual numbers were better. Since 2007, 91 percent of annual revenue and 87 percent of annual customers came back each year. This meant that 87 percent of customers from a year before remained customers the next year, and 91 percent of the revenue that came from a customer one year came from that same customer the next year. Median customer tenure was greater than 15 years. I personally ran the analysis. This is a rare example of the reality of a business being better than advertised: 91 percent vs. 85 percent.

With one business I bought, zero percent of revenue was recurring at purchase. It was quite a pain at times because there was a purchase order (PO) process to go through. In addition, most customers paid via check. While not gold-standard recurring revenue, it was repeat revenue. After purchase, I moved the customers to formal, contractual service agreements (without price caps, of course) to optimize operations and make the business more attractive to a future buyer, enabling me to reduce the need for POs, or at least get POs that would cover multiple years of service. I also moved the majority of our customers from checks to ACH payments. There are no fees for paying ACH, and it saves significant office time.

As with high margins, recurring and/or repeat revenue provides a cushion for an inexperienced operator. With a long service history, customers will tolerate a few hiccups or, in some unfortunate cases, more than a few hiccups, and still stay loyal. This idea was proven later when we were demoing field service management software, and we dispatched the truck to the wrong house of corrections (jail) when responding to an emergency call that was curtailing operations. The forty-five minutes it took to get to the right location was not a happy time.

The same logic applies to customer concentration. If there is a broad base of customers without concentration, then mistakes with a few customers are digestible, whereas if a few customers can make or break the business, an operator may be in for a world of pain if they lose one.

Losing a customer can be caused by an exogenous factor that is out of the operator's control. For example, one of the few customers the industrial services business lost was a food manufacturer that was consolidating operations. The customer was doing well, and the move was only on the radar for a year before being executed. They hired a consultant, a recommendation was made, and the plan was put in place. Our customer contact was as surprised as we were. We did a final servicing, and then they were gone. No skin off my back, though, because, as I'd learned while researching, the business had a fragmented customer base.

I prefer businesses that have a cushion of repeat or recurring revenue and a fragmented customer base. When running a business, failure is one building block for success, and it is optimal to operate with space to learn.

Cash Is King

After school, I was researching jobs at The Federal Bureau of Investigation (FBI), and an agent and I were discussing investigative best practices. When discussing bank robberies, he said the key is following the cash. While I obviously didn't end up taking a job with the FBI, this lesson translates to being an EBO as well. Repeat revenue, a fragmented customer base, ACH payments, purchase orders, being in demand, and everything else we have discussed so far are all factors in the cash equation. It is all fun and games until there is no cash in the bank, payroll is missed, loan payments are missed, and the personal guarantee police come calling. Fifty percent-plus margins and high membership retention are great on paper, but they are meaningless until the cash is in the bank. Cash pays the bills—both in business and in life.

A cash-rich business is king, and ample access to cash to weather a storm or fund an opportunity is always critical. In 2009, I knew that a fitness club was going to be a slam dunk independent of the recession. The challenge was that I needed some cash to get the club open. Lending was extremely tight, and time was of the essence. I used the cash flows from my successful clubs to finance the new clubs and was able to open before someone else took the market. In addition, when COVID-19 hit the clubs, forcing them to close before the Paycheck Protection Program was dispersed, there was ample liquidity to continue paying the bills because cash was plentiful. Focusing on cash generation every day will make a plethora of future problems go away.

Industrial Services Example

Let's look in more detail at the industrial services business to better understand the Double Diamond and the DNA of strong demand (what makes up strong demand). The business sported an amazing historical demand story; the numbers told a compelling tale. The business had:

- grown at an average annual rate of 5 percent per year since 2007
- an 87 percent repeat customer rate since 2007
- a 91 percent repeat revenue rate since 2007
- grown during the great recession from 2007 to 2010
- a fragmented customer base without any serious customer concentration (i.e., the top five customers accounted for less than 25 percent of revenue and the top ten less than 40 percent)

- long-term customers (i.e., nine of the ten top customers had been customers for over twenty years)
- diverse revenue streams (i.e., the largest single business line—grease trap pumping—was less than a third of revenue and the work was recession-resistant)
- customers spread across a variety of industries, including recession-resistant industries such as healthcare, government, education, and critical manufacturing

Customers	
Concentration	9
Sustainability	9.5
Power	9.5
Plan Z	9.5
Score	37.5
Percentage (divided by 40)	93.75%

To boot, the cool places in town were all customers: the professional baseball team, the basketball team, the famous companies, and almost all the good restaurants in town (at least the ones I liked). The company was obviously an important contributor to the community. As I came to learn, providing good service to a food-service establishment often leads to a free meal!

The business was also a safe risk because the industry wasn't going through major changes. In 2019, I was willing to wager with bankruptcy that in the next ten years (the term of my personally guaranteed SBA 7a loan) the core service of exhaust cleaning and pumping would not experience significant innovation or automation. I think the technology that is likely to exist in the future is what has withstood the test of time. The fork, for example, has been around since the fourth century, and my prediction is that it will be around for the foreseeable future. The technology of the core service offerings of the business had not significantly changed since 1987 when the company was founded. The model is technicians in trucks doing dirty, physical, and handy work using rudimentary tools. It is beautiful in its simplicity and timelessness. There was no immediate pipeline of technology under development to disrupt it. Moving the business to the cloud, utilizing routing, and helping technicians do their jobs better with technology assists offered low-hanging fruit for operational improvements to drive profitability and stay ahead of competitors. Yet for the core offerings, change has historically happened at a pace slightly faster than glaciers moving. I knew that if and when innovations happened, I would probably be driving them. I love businesses like this.

Using the Double Diamond on customers, concentration was a 9, sustainability was a 9.5, power was a 9.5, and Plan Z was a 9.5, for 37.5/40—a 93.75 percent.

For the opportunity overall, here is what the Double Diamond looked like. Because the overall score was above 80 percent and the lowest above 60 percent, I was comfortable moving forward.

	Customers	Competitors	Team	Suppliers
Concentration	9	9	7	8
Sustainability	9.5	8	7	6
Power	9.5	8	8	6
Plan Z	9.5	10	9.5	9
Score	37.5	35	31.5	29

	Customers	Competitors	Team	Suppliers
Percentage (divided by 40)	93.75%	87.5%	78.75%	72.5%
Grade	A	B	C	C
Total	83.13%			
Lowest	72.5%			
Go Forward	YES			

How to Conduct Business Research and Diligence

To illustrate how to research a market, we are going to discuss opening a fitness club. The business research and diligence process typically takes months and involves everything from understanding the business' financials to assessing future growth opportunities and risks, as you've seen already. Fitness is a growing industry with significant tailwinds, and in 2008, Anytime Fitness was a leading concept within the industry, especially in fringe markets with limited competition.

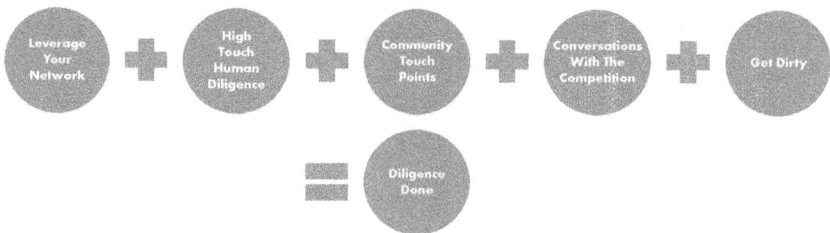

Leverage Your Network

Networking matters. I prioritized networking with other Anytime

Fitness owners. It was a great investment of time. While I preferred spending time with some club owners more than others, I always benefited from the conversation. The idea to open a fitness center in the city came from a neighboring club owner. Maren had been in the fitness industry for years and knew the game, which is the importance of sales and retention. Her approach was high-volume, money upfront, and low dues that made it painless to let the charges continue even in the case of lower-than-planned usage (a common theme in the fitness industry). Maren had a lot going on, and while she was happy to meet with me, it was not high on her priority list.

Upon arrival, one of her employees instructed me to wait. When we finally connected, we sat in her office. She appeared to be in her early thirties and was dressed in jeans, boots, and a North Face fleece. Noticeably, she wasn't wearing any Anytime Fitness or athletic attire. After exchanging pleasantries, we talked about sales, pricing, the franchise, equipment, and the industry. The conversation turned to expansion opportunities.

"What markets do you like?" I gently inquired.

"The town twenty miles south is a great market for a club. I would love to open there at some point, but I am slammed here. You should go after it, as my members would love a club down there," she responded.

The conversation lasted fifteen minutes. She apologized and indicated that she was very busy, saying she wished she had more time. I had been kicked to the curb, yet I was ecstatic. Our conversation was direct and valuable. Armed with the tip, I was off to the races to understand more about the other town.

Located twenty-six and a half miles south and boasting a population of 23,647, the town was ground zero for the Great Recession. Later, in January 2010, the unemployment rate was 15.5 percent;[19] home

19 | *labormarketinfo.edd.ca.gov/cgi/dataanalysis/ labForceReport.asp?menuchoice=LABFORCE*

prices were plummeting, and foreclosures were skyrocketing. A leading newspaper rated it as one of the top twenty hardest-hit communities in California during the Great Recession. But in 2008 and 2009, even as the world was slipping into the financial crisis, it was a gold mine waiting to happen.

A quick search of Google maps showed three competitors: Central Fitness, a mom-and-pop club run by Raymond; Town Fitness, a second mom-and-pop club without a website; and Curves. As I calculated no-traffic drive times between the clubs, it became evident that there were no other fitness options within a twenty-minute drive. In addition, all these clubs were on the west side of the freeway, which comprised around half the city's population. The other half appeared to be mine for the taking, and my gut told me these competitors were not going to be a problem.

High-Touch Human Diligence

Finding a market with a minimal amount of competition is a critical success factor for Anytime Fitness. There was limited competition in the old part of town, and there was no competition on the new side of town. So that is where my research began. I walked around the local supermarket on a weekday and struck up conversations with people in the aisles. I always purchase items from the stores so that I am a paying customer, and the checkout staff are also another good source of information. I built rapport around a shared interest, typically food items, and then steered them toward fitness. People are generally happy to talk and be helpful.

"I would be interested if you open," one customer told me. "I work in corrections and have an odd schedule, so I really need twenty-four-hour access. I currently drive south to work out (twenty-five minutes away), but I almost never go. I feel bad about getting away from my routine after talking with you."

My next stop was It's A Grind, the local coffee shop, for conversations with individuals who made the fateful choice to sit by me.

"Would you pay $40 per month for access to a nice treadmill and weights with 24/7 access?" I asked a soccer mom who had sat next to me as she was drinking an iced mocha and snacking on chocolate bread. (By the way, chocolate bread became my favorite treat from It's A Grind—it is amazing!). Her husband was a farmer.

"I would," she told me. "My husband probably would probably join as well. He is tired of driving north (twenty minutes away) to work out. You should open a club."

Not all conversations were roses, and the rejection was deflating. Certain individuals were turned off by my energy and treated me like a solicitor (which I was) by either waving me off or telling me they were "not interested" before I had a chance to unleash my rapport-building abilities on them, while others explained that not offering childcare or classes was a deal-breaker. Despite these small negative interactions, I spoke with over 100 prospective members over three days (at different times and locations), and the overall feedback was overwhelmingly positive. Word travels fast in small towns, and I was sure word was getting around that a fitness club may be coming to town. The other club owners have me to thank for their sleepless nights of tossing and turning.

Paying for a formal third-party survey can also be a great option, either online, on the phone, or in person.

As an EBO who will be held accountable for the results of my endeavors, I prefer to have the conversations myself. I like to experience the feelings: is the community excited or apathetic? How much demand is there? If I live by my desk, I will die by my desk.

Community Touchpoints

Justin, a senior city employee and resident, was excited about a fitness center coming to town. He saw no government blockers. He indicated he was a "maybe" to getting back to the gym, but that his wife would give it a hard look. Alice, the president of the Chamber of Commerce, thought it was a great option for the new side of town. She bluntly stated that she would stick with Raymond's mom-and-pop club; however, if I really wowed her, she would add a second membership.

"The only thing I can wow you with is my charm," I said, and she chuckled. "Is there any reason I should not open that you are not telling me?"

"You know your business better than me. I think a lot of people will be interested," she said with no delay.

"Advice or things I should keep in mind?" I asked.

"Get involved in the community, which it sounds like you are already planning to do," was her response. She invited me to attend a future Chamber of Commerce meeting.

Justin and Alice were both bullish. Be careful to diligently look for reasons to do things, and also reasons not to do things, to minimize the effects of the numerous biases that plague our thinking, including confirmation bias.[20] In addition, as an outsider coming into a tight-knit community, you need to know as much of what you don't know as possible. By doing this on-the-ground reconnaissance, you can begin to build allies and flip as many enemies to frenemies as possible. Knowledge and networks were power, especially as I already knew other potential hawks were circling to open a fitness center in the future.

Conversations with the Competition

As an EBO, you will need to do the uncomfortable and get to know your competitors intimately.

20 |*Kahneman, Daniel. Thinking, Fast and Slow (Farrar, Straus and Giroux, 2013)*

Local competition

I reached out to Raymond, the owner of Central Fitness, to introduce myself and inquire about getting together. I called his clubs and left messages with his staff, saying I was a club owner looking to connect. I called every four to five days. He ignored me for a few weeks. Eventually he called me back, and I suggested lunch. He said he would think about it. He called me back two weeks later and finally agreed to meet with me. After introductions and ordering, the crucial conversation began.

"I prayed on whether or not to meet with you," he stated.

"I appreciate your taking the time," I said after an awkward silence, unsure how to respond.

"God has brought you into my life for a reason," he replied.

My gut told me that he had a strong sense of right and wrong. He knew the risks of having this conversation. He asked me about Anytime Fitness, and I stated I was interested in acquiring clubs. We talked about markets and competitors. Unprompted, he then said something interesting: "The new side of town could probably use a fitness club."

The owner of the main competitor in town had just told me that demand existed in my target market. Perhaps he determined a new club was inevitable and that I would be a better competitor than the alternatives. Aside from his wife and God, I do not think he'd talked a lot about this with other people.

We finished lunch and mutually promised to keep in touch. I liked Raymond; he was a solid guy. The way he talked left me with the impression that he cared about the community. The country needs more people like him.

For weeks, the owner of Town Fitness didn't return my inquiries. I even visited his club to no avail. Eventually, he called me back and agreed to meet. I said I was interested in buying his club. He had heard

I was thinking about opening a club on the other side of town and was excited for me and for the community to get another fitness option.

I met him and his wife at his club. He was going out of business due to unfortunate personal circumstances. I was interested in buying his club. After mutually determining that a sale did not make sense given the circumstances, he agreed to help me to get my club open in any way he could. He believed the community needed it. He was 100 percent confident I was going to do well on that side of town and wanted to give his members an alternative to Raymond. Another piece of the puzzle was coming together.

Prospective competition

Marcus Winters has been a fitness equipment sales rep at the same company for his entire career. Marcus is reliable and above board. Being career-focused and customer-centric, he had developed good relationships with his network of club owners. At this point in my career, I was in my early twenties, and I had high aspirations in the fitness industry. I purchased fitness equipment from him for my first club. From our very first meeting, I branded myself as someone looking to open and/or purchase additional clubs. Marcus heard this story a lot. In the beginning, he was hesitant to introduce me to his network. Why would he? A lot of new faces came and went in the industry, especially in the franchise space. I stayed persistent, and an opportunity presented itself.

Scott Tellmer was a multi-unit club owner in the California Central Valley. He had been in the industry for over twenty-five years and had opened seven clubs in total. He was looking to unload an underperforming club not far from one of mine. There was alignment: Scott was looking to sell, and I was looking to buy, so a connection made sense.

Scott invited me to his compound, which was in the middle of no-where. He had bought land in an unincorporated area, built a house, and was living in isolation, perhaps waiting for the urban sprawl that is the California Central Valley to continue growing, leading to land appreciation. Either that or he was preparing for Armageddon.

I arrived on a Sunday morning; Scott met me at the door. He was around six feet tall, compact, lean, and with pep in his step. He was sporting an athletic tank top and jeans. He had a solid puff to his up-per body that spoke of disciplined resistance training and a smart diet. The compound was utilitarian and manly like his fitness clubs, a few of which I had visited over the past week. We discussed his club for sale.

"Why are you looking to sell?" I asked.

"To focus on my other clubs," he nonchalantly replied. "It is a great opportunity for someone who is young and hungry."

I eventually visited his club, spent a few days with the staff, and determined that it was not the right fit. A good, but not great, oppor-tunity. What really intrigued me, though, was the idea of expansion.

"What markets do you like?" I asked Scott.

He mentioned the market I was looking at.

"Why?" I asked.

"Raymond has the only other operation in town. I will offer to buy his club and then open mine in the industrial part of town. 24/7 Mon-day through Wednesday, swimming, $50 per month, and classes. No skin off my back if he refuses; I can put him under. Just easier without him there. I will pay him a fair price and keep his staff on. I am focus-ing on my current operations now and will get there eventually," he re-sponded in a tone that implied none of this should be a surprise to me.

I thanked Scott for his time, said I would go to his club next week, and we parted ways. I left his compound feeling lukewarm about his club for sale but excited like a kid in a candy shop about the market

I was pursuing. Even if Scott came to town in a few years, I would be presented with a workable exit option by selling to him.

Between the customers, competitors, and the community, I was confident that there was ample demand. I needed around 400 recurring members to break even and 620 to produce a cash flow of $10,000 per month. I was confident I would get there, and I was highly confident that I could greatly exceed that number. I rated customers at 36/40 using the Double Diamond. Concentration was a 9.5 because members would be pulled from a variety of areas in the city, and no single constituency would represent an overwhelming number of members. For example, if agriculture got hit hard due to a commodities crisis and farmers dropped their memberships, then the club would be fine because we also planned to get a lot of government employees, corrections officers, and teachers as members. Sustainability was a 9.5 as well, since fitness is likely to continue to experience growth, and even though the town was mired in a recession, its long-term growth prospects (linked to the urban sprawl of the surrounding area) were strong. Power was at 7.5; in fitness, attrition is a challenge. To protect against attrition, I planned to invest heavily in culture, ACH payments, long-term agreements, and, most importantly, getting deeply involved in the community. Plan Z was a 9.5. I knew that, if needed, I could staff the club full-time, get involved in the community, and get the club to have enough members to generate strong cash flow. My current business was under stable management, and I even had a family member who could fill the gap in case of an unforeseen event. I felt 36/40, or 90 percent, good about the customers.

All this business research occurred before I had signed a franchise agreement or a lease. I was also doing similar research in half a dozen other markets. Once a commitment to open is made, the ballgame is about execution. Execution is about focus. Regrets or open loops[21] about business research I should have done are a distraction to execution. Distractions are the devil as EBOs seek to achieve their goals.

Action Item

Remember to look for a minimum 80 percent score on the Double Diamond for the opportunity as a whole and no less than 60 percent for any one component. You will want to have a number of viable opportunities in your pipeline, as many of them will fall through.

Visit www.reidtileston.com/grititdone to run some prospective opportunities.

21 | Kelly Forrister, "GTD Best Practices: Collection (Part 1 of 5)," GTD, October 18, 2011, gettingthingsdone.com/2011/10/gtd-best-practices-collect-part-1-of-5/

CHAPTER 4

FINANCING YOUR BUSINESS

If the opportunity is good, the money will follow. Most people think fundraising is the most challenging part of buying a business. In reality, finding a good opportunity is the most challenging part.

A great opportunity on its own isn't enough. Money talks. You need to have the cash to follow through. This chapter will provide a road map for raising the necessary funds to be a low-risk EBO. It will discuss how to use SBA (Small Business Administration) lending programs, as well as options to fill the equity gap. While the money required to be an EBO does not grow on trees, getting financed is easier than most aspiring business owners realize.

Small Business Administration Lending: the 511

Effective EBOs utilize the SBA lending programs. SBA loans are designed to help owner-operators acquire a business. They come with an unconditional personal guarantee, which means that if you default, the bank will come after your personal assets.

The flagship product is the SBA 7a loan program. Under this program, US taxpayers guarantee 75 to 85 percent of the loan that a private lender makes, allowing the lender to take more risk than they otherwise might.[22] In case of default, taxpayers are on the hook for 75 percent. SBA 7a deals can have an interest rate that is typically prime (a daily interest rate) + a spread (an increase that reflects risk; the higher the spread, the riskier) and are often floating. Typically, a 7a deal finances between 60 percent and 90 percent of the total project costs. There is a $5 million cap on the total amount of SBA financing an individual can attain. Base case deals I see are 80 percent SBA financed, with a mix of seller financing (a loan to the buyer) and a buyer equity injection (down payment). Deals are getting done with as little as a 5 percent equity injection from the buyer.

A buyer for one of my fitness clubs used the SBA 7a program, and I have also used it to purchase businesses. Getting a loan made more financial sense than putting in my own equity. In 2018, I was looking at buying FedEx routes. The broker introduced me to a lending team that would underwrite FedEx routes via SBA 7a. The leader of this team is Kevin Goodman, or "King Kevin" as I would come to call him. FedEx routes rely on three-year service agreements that are renewed with very high frequency. However, SBA 7a loans are for ten years. Lenders are hesitant to underwrite ten-year loans when the only source of revenue is a service agreement that expires every three years.

---

22 | *The SBA will guarantee 85 percent of loans less than $150,000 and 75 percent for loans greater than $150,000. Details can be found here: sba.gov/partners/lenders/7a-loan-program/types-7a-loans*

SBA lenders shied away from FedEx deals for that reason. Kevin saw future deal flow, analyzed the rate of FedEx route renewals, looked at the underlying trends of the business, and made the compelling case to his superiors that they should underwrite these deals with SBA 7a financing. They agreed. There are no problems in life, only solutions.

While the FedEx deal did not close, I was impressed with Kevin. He knew how to get things done. When I had a signed letter of intent (LOI)—a non-binding offer to purchase a business that sets out the terms and conditions of the sale—for a business I was considering buying, I engaged Kevin and a few other SBA lenders I had kept in contact with. Certain lenders did not want to underwrite the deal. Others told me, "There is no way you will get a fixed rate for the life of the loan in this environment." The three top offers I eventually got are outlined below.

Here is an overview of the terms that will help you understand the offers. The prime rate, or prime lending rate, is an interest rate used by banks—usually the interest rate at which banks lend to customers with good credit. Variable interest rates may be expressed as a percentage above the prime rate. Essentially, the increase over the base prime rate is an indication of how risky the bank views your opportunity; the higher the spread (increase above prime), the riskier it is. At the time of writing, the maximum allowable spread is 5 percent for SBA loans greater than $250,000. Floating rates mean that as the prime rate changes, the interest rate on the loan changes as well, both up and down. Project costs are the all-inclusive costs associated with the opportunity, including the value of the business or license, working capital, lending fees, rent deposits, and professional feels, etc.

- 75 percent of project costs with an interest rate of prime + 2.5 percent floating (8 percent at the time)

- 80 percent of project costs with an interest rate of prime + 1.75 percent floating (7.25 percent at the time)
- 85 percent of project costs with a fixed interest rate of 5 percent for the life of the loan from King Kevin

Kevin's was the best by a wide margin. All the lenders knew the business, knew me, and knew the risks. Kevin was able to come through in fine fashion. There was risk to my offering. I'd owned businesses for twelve years. All my liquid net worth was going into the down payment and working capital; I owned no other property, and the business I was purchasing had limited collateral. It was an airball (lower than ideal collateral) deal, as they like to say in the SBA world. King Kevin got it done.

Another SBA program is the SBA 504 program, which allows existing businesses to purchase real estate for 10 percent of total project costs down, with a twenty-five-year term and (as of writing) at an interest rate of around 5.75 percent. The remaining 90 percent is provided by an SBA lender and a Certified Development Corporation (CDC).[23] The sum includes total project costs encompassing land acquisition, tenant improvements/construction, and possibly equipment. Aside from family, it is the best lending program I have ever seen. In addition, you can also sublease a portion of the property. When pursuing your opportunity, I strongly encourage you to have a three-year lease with three-year options so that purchasing property is possible without the anchor of an existing lease. Acquiring a business with an SBA 7a loan and then acquiring property with a 504 loan is a recipe for wealth generation.

So why is this the 511 on SBA loans? 7+504 equals...you guessed it!

23 | *"504 Loans," US Small Business Administration, July 26, 2023, ba.gov/funding-programs/ loans/504-loans*

A critical factor in SBA lending is that there is limited oversight from the lender. Make your payments, keep your insurance active, and send them financials (it is not uncommon for lenders to be lax in enforcing this), and they will leave you alone to focus on operations. Not having to spend time dealing with lenders, investors, or a board can free you up to focus on operations. This is heaven on earth for an EBO. Achieving results is contingent on being able to focus, so having a hands-off source of capital can be a significant value-add.

How to De-Risk an SBA Personal Guarantee

The term "personal guarantee" refers to an individual's legal promise to repay credit issued to a business. Providing a personal guarantee means that if the business becomes unable to repay the debt, the individual assumes personal responsibility for the balance. The SBA requires an unconditional personal guarantee from a buyer, which is a hard pill to swallow. If a business defaults on the SBA debt, the borrower is personally liable, which means the lender can come after your house if you are a homeowner. If you do not have the assets to cover the balance, the lender can place you in bankruptcy. You can de-risk an SBA personal guarantee by being thoughtful about which SBA lender you work with. Take a step back and envision that the plan has gone awry. Plan Z failed, all that can go wrong with your business has gone wrong and then, amazingly, even more manages to go wrong. At your lowest moment in life, who is going to be there to take your call? For that matter, will anyone be there to take your call? At least one person will: an attorney who represent clients when they default on SBA loans.

While researching SBA loans, I looked for a guide who would be able to walk me through the default process. The SBA was not much use, and the lenders themselves gave vague answers; the default attorneys were the key.

There is a spectrum among SBA lenders, while the process of default is byzantine. The key takeaway is that certain banks will throw the book at borrowers, while others will work with them to avoid foreclosure, liquidations, bankruptcy, and other undesirable outcomes. The bank I was working with was going to throw the book at me with extra velocity if I defaulted. The outcome was crystal clear to me: if I messed up this opportunity, I was going to declare Chapter 11, and my excellent credit score was going to translate into an excellent opportunity for improvement. My prospective lender had a reputation for being aggressive. I have heard stories of small business borrowers defaulting on one loan with them and then having them invoke the penalty clause on any other lending instruments, charging the maximum interest allowable on, for example, business and personal credit card debt. A twist of the knife in trying times! I am sure this clause was mentioned in the seventy-page loan documents I eventually signed. I respect them for holding borrowers accountable. Accountability is good, especially when taxpayers' money is on the line.

Other banks are more likely to work with the borrower on haircutting the loan (reducing the payments and/or forgiving a portion of the balance) and steering clear of draconian measures like bankruptcy and taking possession of homes.

With the Small Business Administration, Persistence Pays

Alicia Rodriguez personifies what makes America great. She immigrated from Puerto Rico, put herself through school, and got a job with the State of California. Her significant other, Terry, had ten years of experience successfully running fitness clubs, and Alicia saw a path to lift them both up the socioeconomic ladder by buying him his own club. Using an SBA 7a loan to purchase a fitness club presented a great opportunity. It was 2012. By that point, I was ready to sell a few clubs and head off to business school. The kicker is that while Alicia and Terry had enough money for their down payment and had the requisite experience, Terry had a background issue that would preclude him from getting an SBA 7a loan. The deal was a good one for them: 75 percent SBA financing; 10 percent downpayment, and 15 percent seller note (when the seller agrees to accept a portion of the purchase price in a series of deferred payments).

Alicia was ready for a fight: when the SBA came back rejecting their application, she dug in, appealed the rule that prevented them from getting the loan, and won an exception with the SBA. Persistence pays. I have observed lots of parties give up when faced with similar SBA hurdles, but not Alicia. She powered forward and ended up closing on the club. It was a great business at a fair price. She and Terry were able to purchase the club. Alicia paid the seller note in full, on time, and with no complaints. Alicia is inspirational.

Equity, Debt, and Governance

Owning your upside is a compelling reason to be an EBO. Taking on outside equity from investors minimizes your personal upside by diluting ownership. Here's a simple example: if you give investors 30 percent of the equity/ownership in a business, they will own 30 percent of the profits and 30 percent of the sale proceeds. In addition, they may also mandate interest payments on the equity and require that their equity is paid back before you receive your equity payments. Whereas with 100% ownership, once you pay off your debt, all of the upside will be yours". While investors provide money and other intangible value, EBOs should be thoughtful about giving up equity. Let's remember the Golden Rule: those with the gold make the rules. Taking on outside equity means that operators are giving up a level of control and upside.

Value-Add Equity

When my first fitness club was struggling, I had two equity partners who were employed full-time; they had limited ability to be helpful on the ground, yet they ultimately controlled the company. They had all kinds of brilliant suggestions but a limited ability or desire to actually get involved and be helpful.

"We are getting hammered by a lack of sales. We are just not hitting our numbers," I said. "We do not have money for marketing. I am just going to keep pounding the pavement with guerilla marketing."

"Good idea. Let us know how we can be helpful," Ty responded.

"Come out here and help me sell," I said.

"I cannot do that," was the response.

"Understood," I sadly stated.

Sensing that I was not happy with the end result of the conversation and still striving to be helpful, Ty sent me a book on sales using company funds. I suppose it is the thought that counts. Rationally, the investors focused on their careers and other income-generating activities. They had capped personal liabilities in this endeavor, so once the liabilities were stabilized, they focused elsewhere and left me to grit it done. I had signed up for this and would take my medicine.

Little did I know a superhero would rescue me! In the sweltering summer heat, I rented a purple superhero suit from the franchisor. Captain Running Man was a full-body costume with big muscles, a cape, shoes, and boots. It was an attention-grabber. Then I pounded the pavement with a special offer for customers: a three-month, summertime, paid-in-full membership to generate cash to stabilize the business. I also added auto-renewals with electronic payments to help drive the recurring membership dues thereafter.

Using the Running Man suit was a tried-and-true page out of the sales playbook. It generated buzz!

I would take it to a whole new level over the years to come. There was a Trader Joe's next door to the club I frequented. I was going to wear the Running Man suit over there.

When the suit arrived at the club, I went to the back storage closet to put it on. My dad had recently bought me a bottle of limoncello, which I had in the club. I decided some liquid courage might help, taking a swig here and there as I got ready. I was able to get the suit on, but I needed help with the back zippers, just like a girl getting ready for a big night on the town. *What is my life coming to?* I wondered. I had to ask Bobby, the club manager, to help zip it up. Not wanting to be seen on the club floor just yet, I called Bobby on his cellphone.

Bobby is your average hetero male who has worked in construction. Seeing his boss donning a purple superhero suit evoked a mixed reaction of awkwardness and admiration.

"Wow! You are really doing this," he said.

"Oh yeah," I said with enthusiasm. "Can you zip me up?"

"Of course," he said, zipping up both the muscle suit and the outer purple layer.

Now buzzed from the booze, I saw no need to continue to wait around. I made my appearance on the club floor, my heart pounding and my vision blurry.

"Here he is, ladies and gentlemen! It is Captain Running Man!" Bobby proclaimed, without having to be asked.

"It is great to meet you. Today is a great day to work out!" I said as I handed out high fives and handshakes.

"Reid?" one member inquired.

"Captain Running Man, your local fitness superhero motivating the community to get active. It's a great day to work out!" I shot back in a robotic monotone reminiscent of a *Star Trek* droid.

I was nervous and scared but on my game. The real adventure waited outside. The corner where the club was located is a busy intersection, visited by over 70,000 cars per day. Waiting to cross the street, I was met with horns and a few fist pumps. I was elated. At this point, it was hot—ninety-plus degrees. The light flipped, and it was my time to cross. My destination was the Trader Joe's across the street. I was looking forward to the AC as much as I was fearing people's reactions. When I walked in, the staff in the elevated office area looked at me, instantly rang the Trader Joe's bell, and started clapping. Positive contagion kicked in and more people started clapping.

"Captain Running Man from Anytime Fitness. Your local fitness superhero. Today is a great day to work out!" I exclaimed.

I was riding high from the energy boost. I walked the aisles, introducing myself and the club. I grabbed a free sample and a healthy wrap for lunch. Captain Running Man paid with a credit card. Silently waiting in the checkout line was awkward.

"It was epic!" I responded before being asked when I got back to the gym.

Being a superhero is empowering. Donning a full-body muscle suit is the ultimate form of an Amy Cuddy power pose. Dressing down brought back memories of a hangover. I was having my mojo taken away.

Captain Running Man would make more trips that summer, even as the heat index crept up. Starbucks, the local Mexican joint, and the grocery store were added as critical stops. We tracked lead sources, and Captain Running Man worked. Pure euphoria ensued whenever a new member enrolled that I remembered from the Captain Running Man suit. It built club culture.

Most equity investors are not going to come out and wear a purple superhero suit in the sweltering heat like an EBO will when the going gets tough.

The whole experience drilled into me the difference between an equity employee and an owner. As a business owner, the buck stops with you; the owner is ultimately responsible. When membership sales are down, the owner will be the one in the superhero suit. A CEO is an equity employee who may not have the same motivation.

The years 2007 and 2008 forged my identity as a business owner. Understanding your entrepreneurial identity is critical. I had mine at the tender age of twenty-four. EBOs understand whether they are an equity employee or a business owner. Both offer amazing opportunities; the self-awareness to recognize which one is the right fit is critical.

The next step for me would be transitioning from a business owner to an EBO.

Investors

You may be able to use your own money to fill the gap of an SBA loan, in which case you will not need investors. Alternatively, you may also choose to raise money from investors and share in the upside. Finding and managing investors takes time. Investors will require a return on their capital, and you will have to create fundraising documents and projections that outline this. To attract investment to an opportunity in the ETA space, prospective operators should show an IRR, which is the annual growth rate that the investment is expected to generate, of at least 30%. This means you will need a credible plan to profitably grow the business. When you have a good opportunity that can credibly generate that kind of return, investors will flock to you. Follow the guidance from Chapters 1 to 3.

There's one important question to ask: what value might investors add to my business? Equity is valuable, and giving it up should be a thoughtful discussion. Good reasons run the gamut. Investors can mentor operators, help with critical strategic decisions, provide a buffer against the loneliness of operating, and provide cash and accountability. Oftentimes, investors are current or past operators who "get it." Those with industry expertise can provide useful insights into the market and operations, and they can provide valuable networking opportunities. Those with transactional expertise can add value during an exit, and investors provide a valuable pipeline for future opportunities. The key is to decide whether investors are the right strategy to fill those needs or if an equity partner, investment banker, loan, equity employee, or a peer group board of directors are the better fit. Effective EBOs reserve equity for those who are able to add value to the enterprise beyond financials. Personally, I am greedy with equity. It is a sacred gift allocated to those who can help the business.

How to Cultivate Investor Relationships

Having pre-existing investor relationships is not mandatory. Adam was a searcher who sourced a fleet-management company at a reasonable multiple through a proprietary channel. It scored high on the Double Diamond. Once the deal was under exclusive LOI, he shopped it to outside investors, was able to raise the equity (including from me) that he needed to close, and got the deal across the finish line. The merits of your opportunity and your background will speak for themselves. In addition, if you are unable to find a viable opportunity, having all the best investor relationships in the world will not help you with your goal. With that said, diligence and fundraising is a busy time made easier by having long-standing relationships with your investor base. Cultivating investors and keeping them in the loop with your opportunities will allow both parties the time to develop a resonant relationship.

Let's look at three examples on the spectrum. Chris, who runs a commercial services business, described his relationship with investors as "a constant struggle that weighs on my physical well-being and is a distraction to growing the business." Tony, who sold a successful residential services business, reflected that "this is just another transaction where, to be frank, investors profited a lot from our hard work and effort." Contrast that with Marcus, who when reflecting on his exit said, "I owe this return to my investors for backing me, supporting me, and helping me navigate tough times." A healthy operator-investor relationship has the potential to span beyond your first deal into future opportunities. After a successful exit from a light manufacturing business, Jack went on to make his next career managing the money of one of his high net-worth investors. My recommended best practice is to cultivate ten investor relationships before your search, send quarterly life/search updates, and share deals for their feedback at the signed LOI stage. If you want me (through Grit It Done L.L.C.) to invest in your deal, at minimum read this book, follow me on LinkedIn or Twitter, and send me deals that fit the criteria outlined in this book. Bonus points for attending a class I teach or an event I put on and double bonus points for visiting me in person to go for a hike or a cold plunge. All proceeds from this book will be used to fund investments in EBOs.

Board

While most private businesses do not have a board, deciding whether to have one is a critical decision. Board members provide subject matter expertise, diverse opinions, and tangible experience. Board members can be paid or given equity or will sometimes even do it at no cost for the experience and networking. Investors and board members are not the same role. Investors can be board members, but board members do not have to be investors. For a business owner, a board member can be a value-add as an advisory service that brings business ideas and expertise that otherwise would not have been discovered and can add tremendous value. Boards also provide a mechanism for bringing up thorny, long-term issues that are important to discuss. Dennis Kessler, a board member associate, says, "As one of the original founders of the Private Directors Association (PDA), we created PDA to educate private company owners that inclusion of independent directors on private company boards helps the boards deal with issues that the management team is sometimes reluctant to bring up. Since independent directors are not involved in day-to-day operations, they take a long view and help the board stay focused on the strategic issues." Remember, a board can be an "advisory" board that does not require the owner to give up control. For an EBO, the most valuable commodity is time; having a board requires time to manage and organize. So the question of having a board is a matter of time allocation.

Choose Your State Wisely

Be thoughtful about which state you intend to own a business in. Talk to business owners in the state, and browse the business friendliness rankings. Regulations, policies, and attitudes vary widely across states and communities, which will impact your bottom line and your state of mind. For example, California is a hub of technological innovation. The workforce is educated; the weather is fantastic, and the collaborative culture of Silicon Valley is unrivaled. The world is better off because of the entrepreneurial outputs of the Bay Area. I am a believer that the best is yet to come from California. However, California also excels at making it difficult to run a small business!

Action Item

Visit www.reidtileston.com/grititdone to tell us about an instance where you followed through on a personal guarantee.

CHAPTER 5

CLOSE A TRANSACTION

Grit it done! Most people think the hardest part of the deal is negotiating the price. In reality, the hardest part of the deal is managing everyone's emotions—especially your own.

Throughout the courtship and closing process, be credible and stay dedicated to doing the deal. In the case of acquiring an existing business, once you have initially researched the opportunity, you submit an offer, which we'll talk through in the pages to come. If a buyer accepts it, due diligence begins, a formal agreement is signed, and then grit it done to close! The world is binary: either you close on your opportunity or not. This chapter will lead you through the best practices of how to manage relationships to help you close smoothly.

Meet the Seller in Person

An investor friend of mine likes to remind people that even in the twenty-first century and armed with a plethora of technology, deals are often done "at the kitchen table." In-person interactions are critical for building relationships. When I was first considering buying the industrial services business, I met the seller at a BBQ joint for lunch. I arrived first and grabbed a seat. A few minutes later, Frank showed up. He was wearing jeans, work boots, and a company sweatshirt. He looked like a maintenance worker coming in for lunch after a hard morning in the field—an in-your-face reminder that he was an owner-operator who was actively involved in a hands-on business. I would be having a lot of similar experiences to Frank in the coming years.

Having scrutinized the menu beforehand, I had decided on a BBQ ham sandwich so I could focus my attention on the conversation. We spent half the time talking about Frank's passion for hunting and swapped experiences about our time in Alaska. In a sign of money not being a blockade in his life, he noted that he'd paid for his daughter's boyfriend to come along on the trip they had taken there over the summer.

Throughout the conversation, it became clear that Frank had created a highly profitable, hands-on lifestyle business that gave him the flexibility to spend time with his kids and hunt—all while working around thirty hours per week. The downside was that it required him to be all-in and on-call at times. We talked about trucks, operational capacity, demand, and emergency calls. As an EBO, I can easily create rapport with other owners about the usual gripes: managing people, taxes, regulators, and the incessant piles of business mail that can require hours to work through. With the information I had been given access to, I knew the business was fundamentally solid, and I came to the conclusion that I could step into Frank's role. I fell in love with the business over lunch. My heart fluttered like it does after an epic first date; the possibilities seemed endless. The euphoria faded as I gradually came back to Earth. I was fearful that others would likely have the firepower to pay more and offer better terms than I could. I resigned myself to the fact that while the company was a good one, it was bound to get away.

Gift-Giving

Having a strong personal relationship with the seller will help you navigate the emotionally laden and stressful closing process. Gift-giving helps. Qualifying the seller is important to moving the deal forward. Sellers have different utility points and personal quirks, like the rest of us. After meeting Frank, I was determined to create a strong personal relationship with him. My thinking was that while I may not be able to pay the most, I could (at least partially) offset that with strong rapport. In addition, I felt that if Frank liked me, he would be more likely to be honest in our dealings. As Robert Cialdini states in his classic manual *Influence: The Psychology of Persuasion*, being likable is crucial.[24] After our first meeting, I sent him a gift basket of nuts to share with the team, along with a note that said, "I am going nuts about how excited I am about buying your business!"

Throughout the diligence process, I found things to bond with Frank over. At a bachelor party in Nashville, I went to a gun range at the planner's request and did some shooting. I shared the video and experience with Frank to drive a conversation about rounds per minute, his favorite guns, and shooting experiences—including my getting the shotgun and rifle merit badges at Boy Scout camp. After signing the LOI, I bought Frank some Alaskan elk jerky. He had taken a trip to Alaska with his family, which he was fond of talking about and, because he was a hunter, I knew he would appreciate the snack. Gift-giving leads to likeability.

24 | Cialdini, R. B. (2008). *Influence* (5th ed.). Pearson.

Manage an Intermediary Relationship to
Help You Win the Deal

A healthy relationship with the seller's intermediary is a common theme among successful transactions. Christine is an EBO that bought a manufacturing company after a long corporate career in a different industry. She marketed herself by meeting with the intermediary in-person to present her buying credentials and continued to nurture the relationship through closing. The intermediary had so much faith in the business and in Christine that they rolled their fee into equity in the deal.

Because of their independent relationship with the seller, the intermediary is well positioned to help you win the deal. Simon (the intermediary) and I developed a strong relationship. He took more of an interest in my personal life: asking about my significant other, making sure I was getting enough sleep, and preparing me for what I was getting myself into by buying an industrial services business. He would typically start off conversations with a jovial comment such as, "Well, if it isn't the California Kid!" If I was lucky enough to speak first, I would start off the call with, "It is your favorite business owner!" These jokes led to more of a rapport between us.

"Let's get to 'yes.' There are no problems in life, only solutions," I told Simon before submitting the LOI.

"Offer an all-cash deal," Simon said. "That is how you differentiate yourself from the strategics."

Simon was incentivized to get the deal done as quickly as possible at the highest possible price. Despite our rapport, Simon worked for Frank, and that was where his loyalties stood. Simon is Frank's strategic adviser. What Simon thought of me would filter back to Frank and vice versa. Therefore, my talking points to him centered around credibility and a desire to get the deal done. Likeability and rapport would be beneficial to that end. In addition, Simon knew I had limited experience in the industry, and in the case that the business struggled or if I wanted to sell it later, I would probably pick up the phone and give him a call—which I eventually did for an opinion of value in early 2022 when the business was thriving and I was ready to sell.

While Frank was paying Simon, I was paying Frank, so in effect, I was paying Simon. I did my best to think of him as my vendor. What I appreciate about spending time working with someone in intense situations (which buying a business certainly is) is that they can provide effective coaching and feedback. Simon became useful as my strategic adviser when thinking through how to manage the transition and crucial conversations with employees and the lender that would come later.

While Simon and I did not take part in any gift-giving, we certainly had fun getting to know each other. If the metric was enjoying the journey, our relationship was a success.

Establishing Financial Credibility

The broker and seller want to work with a buyer who can close. Gift-giving and rapport-building aside, I came through faster and in more depth than was requested at every step. Before submitting an LOI, I had to establish credibility. They wanted to see personal financial statements showing my net worth—no problem. They also wanted a letter from an SBA lender stating that they will lend to me—already in my possession.

"Just let me know what you need to establish credibility. I am not here to waste anybody's time. Especially my own. Would you like a copy of my credit score and report?" I asked Simon.

"No need," he said.

"That is only one SBA lender. Would you like another letter, or would you like me to arrange a call with a different one so you know I have options?" I asked.

"No need."

Sometimes I made judgment calls and provided information I knew would help build my credibility whether it was requested or not.

"Also, just to be clear, I am going to use the SBA," I added. I am attaching a financial statement from a high-net worth individual to illustrate to you and Frank that if I really want to do this deal, I have access to deep pockets for an equity check."

As Frank and Simon were analyzing buyers, there could be no question about my ability to get the deal done at the price I was proposing. When looking for a business, you will be competing with a plethora of well-financed and experienced parties; it is essential that you put together a compelling buyer story and be persistent.

Submit an Offer

LOIs are often negotiated back and forth. Thanks to my relationship with Simon, I had a good idea of what I needed to offer to win the deal, with regard to both price and terms. I made an aggressive offer and, after some back and forth on the details, I had a signed LOI.

Visit www.reidtileston.com/grititdone to access a sample LOI. Given that you are about to invest resources and money, a period of exclusivity during which the seller cannot have discussions with other buyers is key.

Diligence

Once the terms of an acquisition are agreed to through an LOI, you move past the business research phase, and formal diligence begins. This is when you will begin to really understand the business. Visit www.reidtileston.com/grititdone to access a starter diligence list.

Advisers such as intermediaries, accountants, attorneys, and book-keepers should play a role in diligence. Keep in mind that it will ultimately be you who is running the business post-close, so get as hands-on as possible to understand the inner workings of the business. Diligence lists are quite a task for the seller, and requesting items can strain the relationship as trust is being established. Nevertheless, get everything you need and leave no stone unturned.

My diligence list was sent with the signed LOI and included a number of aggressive asks, including every monthly P&L that they had available (in this case they were available from 2007 onwards). Within two days, Frank had produced everything I had requested. Moving fast ensured I could complete everything I needed to before submitting the asset purchase agreement.

Starter Diligence List

Company and legal information

Formation documents and operating agreements

Detailed ownership information and member register

Details of any other investment or ownership interest in any other entity held by the company

Licenses, permits, or other governmental authorizations necessary to conduct the company's business

Copies of correspondence with government authorities

Detailed list of property owned, leased, or used by the company, including contracts, LOIs, and real estate lease agreements

List and description of intellectual property, including trademarks, service marks, trade names, patents (including expired patents), copyrights, domain names, and any other intellectual property

Detailed information about all litigation, claims, investigations, proceedings, arbitrations, grievances, or other legal procedures in the past, present, or pending

Copies of any contracts or material agreements, including those with vendors and suppliers

Financial information

Reviewed financial statements

Description of accounting methods and treatments

Disclosure of any accounting issues

Historical cash flows

Monthly income statements and balance sheets

Detailed information on indebtedness and financial arrangements, including all related documentation

Monthly bank statements for all accounts, both active and closed

Accounts payable process and procedures

Information on procedures pertaining to banking, cash, and corporate credit cards

Tax documentation

Sales software data with breakdown by product type, sales mix, etc.

If applicable, any documents relating to material write-downs or write-offs

Details of General & Administrative (G&A) expenses for the last three years, such as rent and salary

Merchant account statements and reports

Discussion of accounts payable process and procedures

Banking/cash/corporate credit cards—cash handling procedures; bank account access/authorization; internal controls

User access/login for accounting system(s)

Human Resources

Employment agreements and detailed compensation reports

Detailed org chart, including information on departures of key employees within the last three years

Employee benefit plans and related documents

Biographies for key employees

Operations

Government inspection reports (as applicable to your business)

If applicable, customer satisfaction surveys

Current sales materials describing the company's products/services

If applicable, strategic sales and marketing plans, digital marketing strategies, and marketing planning information

Updates on current business development initiatives

Rationale behind historical pricing and analysis undertaken to determine appropriate increases

Information on anticipated future price increases or adjustments

Detailed information on sourcing and supply chain strategy and operations

Information on any potential supply or inventory problems

Technology

Description of IT systems, current vendors/providers, and any recent/anticipated changes in providers or platforms

If applicable, procedures in place to ensure compliance with data protection legislation

Insurance and liability

List of all material insurance arrangements setting forth insurer, nature of risks covered, insured amounts, and deductibles

Summary of claims experience under insurance policies, including pending claims

All correspondence relating to cancellation or non-renewal of any material insurance policy

All other relevant documents pertaining to the company's insurance and liability exposure

Description of workers' compensation policy, historical experience ratings, and high-level claims information

Remember that what you do not discover during diligence will come back to haunt you post-close. Justin is an EBO who bought a business that was dependent on seasonal labor only to find out that one low-level team member was single-handedly responsible for a large portion of recruitment. This presented a painful supplier concentration challenge to confront. In addition, what you discover during diligence will impact the price you are willing to pay and may even kill the deal. Richard was an EBO who was looking at a staffing company and found out during diligence that there was more customer concentration than advertised. This put the customer Double Diamond score below 60 percent, which caused him to walk away. It was disappointing, but this is what diligence is ultimately for.

You know that you have done diligence correctly when you can teach the seller things they don't know about their business. This is a benefit to the seller as well; with diligence, they are getting a high-priced and thorough consulting engagement done on their business that's paid for by the buyer. The above diligence list is a starter list, and your specific opportunities will require tailored diligence requests.

Getting confident about your diligence requires getting your hands dirty in the financials. In the process of doing diligence on one business, I had bank and credit card statements for the past two years. I had a bookkeeper do a QOE (quality of earnings) report to make sure the numbers aligned. I had every reason to believe her. I also did my own QOE. I took around a dozen hours to look at every check, credit card charge, ACH transaction, and check deposit from the past two years. Theft, fraud, and misrepresentation are rampant in small businesses. Third parties occasionally miss things or make mistakes in diligence. A reputable QOE provider once made a mistake that overstated a company's EBITDA by 15 percent. The mistake was not discovered until after the deal closed. While the seller was happy as a clam having been overpaid, the buyer who had paid for the QOE was not.

I always follow the cash. During diligence for the industrial services business, I uncovered two things. The first was that in the EBITDA calculations, the seller salary had been included, meaning that EBITDA (profitability) had been overstated. The owner and his team reviewed the numbers and came to the same conclusion. I was paying a multiple of EBITDA, and because EBITDA was lower than the agreed purchase price, the price was reduced.

Second, I could not for the life of me figure out why the money that was deposited into the bank was around 5 percent higher than the

P&L numbers. I thought I had discovered missed revenue, and that profitability might be higher than forecast. Was I buying a business that had over 50 percent EBITDA margins? It turned out, I was not; it was just sales tax that the business was collecting.

I could tell from three years of bank and credit card statements that the business was generating a ton of cash. I could even start to see who more of the customers were from names on checks and bank statements. When I entered the business on day one, I had a keen understanding of the cash flow. During the bank underwriting process, the bankers often asked me questions about working capital. Given my thorough level of diligence, I could answer with an unrivaled level of confidence because I had looked over every transaction. Preparation is the currency of confidence.

A Note on Regulatory Culture

Be sure to carefully investigate the business climate in the community you choose to operate in. For example, the industrial services business was regulated by the Department of Natural Resources (DNR). The agency is best known for having sway over deer-hunting permits—but when not allocating permits, they also regulate pumpers. DNR is solution-oriented. They have rules to enforce with the public's interest at heart, and those regulations need to be followed. For example, during the height of the COVID-19 pandemic, Frank's time as operator-in-charge (the person who is responsible for making sure the business is compliant) was coming to an end. I was in line to become operator-in-charge per our transition plan. In order to do that, I had to take a master operator exam, but in-person exams were suspended due to the pandemic. The state had not yet rolled out electronic exams. The business needed an operator-in-charge, and Frank was stepping down. DNR granted a short-term extension and also set up a private examination for me outside in a park by the business. A department representative met me for a private test. Talk about excellent customer service! I passed with flying colors. In addition, DNR instituted a plethora of other COVID-19 policies that were designed to be helpful and solution-oriented. In addition to the actual substance of the policies, they had a tough but fair and supportive attitude. Different states and communities have different regulatory cultures, which will impact both your bottom line and your state of mind.

How to Manage a Site Visit

As part of my diligence process, I wanted to be on-site at the industrial services business for seven straight days if possible. Unfortunately, Frank would only allow me on-site on Sundays for initial diligence. Within two days of signing the LOI, I had my first Sunday wintertime visit arranged. Time kills deals, and (unfortunately) there are a number of factors out of our control that can cause delays. Move with haste whenever possible. I liked the business so far, and I knew I would uncover a lot of interesting items during diligence. I wanted to "fail fast" and uncover any roadblocks as quickly as possible so I could move on. When there was nothing more I could do to make progress, I focused on keeping my other deals alive so as not to fall into the trap of having all of my eggs in one basket—a common pitfall for prospective EBOs. I recommend that you have at least ten businesses you are actively researching while you are engaged in diligence for one business.

Site visits are a great opportunity to continue to grow the relationship with the seller and truly understand the business. The key is to prepare and keep it simple. My first visit came during a terrible blizzard that wreaked havoc on my travel; nevertheless, with good planning and unrivaled resolve, I made it early. Upon arrival, I located the office. Frank gave me a quick tour. He had clearly been doing this a lot with other prospective buyers. He briefly showed me the office manager's desk, a red book, and the disorganization that was the general manager's desk. He then gave me a pair of earplugs and a single glove. He turned on a pumper truck, to show off the power of the vacuum. Following his lead, I put my hand over the valve and felt it suck my hand to the rim with a powerful force. Even with the protection of the glove, my hand hurt upon contact. What impressed me about the operation was that every square foot of the place was filled. It was amazingly efficient. I could easily see how the company had achieved its 45 percent profit margins.

Being in the presence of big trucks, tools, chemicals, grease, grit, and danger brought me to a happy place. This was the kind of place doing the necessary work that keeps the country moving. The operation was powerful in its simplicity, while rugged in its form. Guys get in trucks and do dirty work. No education required, no higher principle at play, no complaints, no unproven technology, just a group of guys gritting it done—and making a ton of money in the process. Places like this make America amazing.

I could not wait to get back there ASAP to continue diligence. Before doing that, I needed to have a signed purchase agreement, which would lay out the terms for continued site visits and employee conversations. I had started to dig into the documents that had been sent over to conduct diligence. Concurrently, I was working with the lender to finalize my business plan and projections. I was neck-deep in diligence.

How to Manage Legal Stress

Legal documents such as LOIs and purchase agreements will strain the relationship between buyer and seller. Deals often fall apart at this stage. Inevitably, issues will arise during diligence and negotiating the legalese that will lead you or the seller to want to walk away.

Controlling your attorney and strategic advisors is key in this process. Surround yourself with advisors who have experience in business acquisitions and are solution-oriented. The rapport building between buyer and seller that happens early in the process can minimize the fallout and help push the deal forward as long as all parties are reasonable. If the relationship is strong enough, it can weather the storm. This is a delicate process. While an attorney's job is to protect their client, there is an important balance to be struck between protection and scuttling a deal. Control what you can. Make sure you have competent and dedicated counsel that will prioritize your deal, including responding in real-time as the process plays out. Kyle is an EBO who, when selling a custom manufacturing business, grew frustrated that his attorney was taking too long and that he had to spend hours reviewing the document for mistakes. He ultimately created the legal documents himself and was able to successfully sell his business to a younger EBO. Remember, time kills all deals, and responding fast as both a buyer and seller builds credibility. It is also important that you invest early in the process by building rapport with the seller. With a strong relationship, you are positioned to prime the seller for the rough road ahead.

Use Your Network

Using your network can help you navigate the tricky waters during diligence. When doing diligence on the industrial services business, I used my extended network to understand an unfamiliar business because I had no experience in the space. Jason Parson has been a restaurant owner for forty years, and I knew him from my fitness club ownership days. He hired industrial service companies for his restaurants in California. When I showed him the opportunity I had, and kept him in the loop with my learnings all the way up to close, he thought it made sense.

"You will add professionalism to what is a dirty business," he said.

That sounded good to me. With 20/20 hindsight, I can say he was spot on with that prediction.

Through searchfunder.com, I was also introduced to a University of Chicago Booth School of Business graduate who had worked for a fund that did acquisitions in the industrial services space. He broke it down for me in no uncertain terms. The ballgame is in the disposal. The pumper with the lowest disposal costs will win out. There are a few strategic buyers in the space who may provide exit options. The capital expenditures can be lumpy, but industrial services businesses can do very well. As I kept him in the loop while I was doing diligence, his analysis was that I had found a good company and should go for it. He gave me the name of the strategic buyers, and then my friend Dan reached out to them. He learned that pumper trucks were replaced after ten years. If they were older than ten years, they were deducted from the purchase price, the general size of the acquisitions that they considered, and a range of the multiples of EBITDA they would pay. This information proved to be useful for buying and selling the business.

Justin is an EBO who was doing diligence on a niche commercial cleaning company that provided a mission-critical service. The company appeared to have a fragmented customer base. When Justin brought on an industry insider to help during diligence, it was discovered that 50% of the revenue was coming from a single payer with multiple locations, and the service provided to that customer was out-side of the mission-critical service scope that the EBO was attracted to. While not a deal killer using the Double Diamond, this discovery led to recalibrating the deal and the post-close action plan.

Discover Areas for Improvement

There are almost always areas for improvement. The industrial services business was very profitable, and there is a lot of wisdom in the saying, "If it ain't broke, don't fix it." When it comes to change, less is more. I like the "two, two, and a half" rule when thinking about operational improvements: it will take twice as long, cost twice as much, and have 50 percent of the expected upside. But there are exceptions to all rules, and I think of these exceptions as low-hanging fruit.

At the industrial services business, the scheduling since 1987 had been done out of a red book. The team would write appointments in pencil as they came in. For a long time with recurring customers, the general manager Tom would write their last service date on an index card that he would use to know when to schedule their next appointment. This system led to a plethora of missed appointments. Over the years, customers started to ask for service schedules for the upcoming year to make sure they made it in the red book. Other customers would proactively call a few weeks before they wanted service. I found it interesting how customers evolved their practices and adapted to the system. Tom would then write the number of hours each job took so that when it came to pricing and quotes for the next year, he could bid intelligently. Most years, Tom would send revised quotes to customers so they could budget for the upcoming years. This system worked and led to 45 percent profit margins, but it was highly inefficient. I knew I could do better.

"You hate the red books, but they work," Tom said.

"I love the red books. They are amazing. And we need to move with the times," was my response.

During diligence, I did indeed come to love the red books. While I scrutinized the billing files the intermediary had sent me, I would take a red book from a random year, look up the date, and test who was still currently a customer. Even from twenty years ago, around 80 percent of the customers in the red book remained customers. The red books offered powerful insights into the business and also represented low-hanging fruit to improve the business. It was good, but the company could do better. Before actually implementing change, it was critical to get in the field and understand how the business actually worked.

When we transitioned from the red book to field service management software (the cloud), I was able to grow revenue and profitability and, in doing so, leave the company better than I found it.

How to Manage the Final Days

The purchase agreement dictated that I could visit with key employees before closing and back away if the conversations did not go as planned. Tom was a key employee, and I wanted him to sign a non-compete to ensure he would not leave for a competitor. Frank was frustrated that my non-compete ask was slowing down the process. Delays so close to the finish line can be deadly! There was no benefit to Tom for signing a non-compete; nevertheless, Tom had told Frank that he would give me a year to see how things went. However, I had to stick to the plan and get a written commitment before closing.

Frank and Tom were pumping grease traps when Frank called. He expressed that Tom was a man of his word and indicated that he would sign the non-compete and stay for a year. Trust, but verify. I needed to hear it from the horse's mouth. I left for the bank to sign the loan documents, but I was stressed and worried until I heard from Tom. Until then, I couldn't focus on anything else. In fact, I made a number of wrong turns on the way to the bank.

Finally, the call came in, and I bolted outside to answer. Tom said he would sign the non-compete and give me at least a year. He was in! I was relieved beyond words. The deal was going to happen. I spewed some positivity his way and ventured back into the bank feeling like a superhero as we finished signing the loan documents. With the final stroke of the pen, we were done. It was full speed ahead; I could feel the happy chemicals circulating my body. With this assurance from Tom, I was happy to waive the key employee conversation clause in the purchase agreement. The next day we would close, and I would meet the rest of the team, who would find out that I was the new owner. At the hotel, I role-played the conversations. The next day was going to be transformational, and I was teeming with anticipation and joy.

Close Day

The finish line was here. There were three high-level objectives for closing day, listed in order:

- Pay Frank
- Meet the team and have nothing go wrong
- Make sure the attorneys did not make any costly clerical mistakes

I had a check for Frank for the equity portion, and the bank was set up to wire the rest. All the bank paperwork was complete, and the processes to close were in place.

I was excited. My two-and-a-half-year quest to find the right opportunity was about to come to a close, and I was set to enter a new chapter. We had haggled over the details of how to tell the team members. For byzantine legal reasons, the team would have to be terminated by Frank and then rehired by me. Frank wanted to place their termination letters in their mailboxes and then have the discussion about being rehired. I pleaded with him to allow me to have conversations with them before receiving their termination letters. Eventually, he relented and agreed.

I arrived and met Frank in his office. He was warm and jovial. He was going to give the news, and then I was going to follow on with business as usual and give them a pile of paperwork to bring back the following day as part of the rehiring process. Exciting times lay ahead!

Action Item

What is a deal you have closed on? Visit www.reidtileston.com/gritidone to share a time you successfully got a deal across the finish line.

CHAPTER 6

DEVELOPING ENTREPRENEURIAL EMPLOYEES

Earn absentee ownership by investing in your people. Most people think that being an absentee owner is the starting point. In reality, this is earned through cultivation of and delegation to entrepreneurial employees.

Former CEO Rich said it well when referring to a common theme of successful small businesses: They were built with the help of a super dedicated team member who freed up the owner to work on optimizing operations so that the business could prosper. It is common knowledge that good people are critical to small businesses. In fact, a single team member with an ownership attitude is often the backbone of the business.

What is an entrepreneurial employee? The litmus test is when customers and suppliers who do not know any better think the employee is the owner of the business. Working with entrepreneurial employees has been one of the most inspiring experiences of my life and of countless other EBOs.

This chapter will provide a framework and real-world examples of how to cultivate entrepreneurial employees and achieve absentee ownership. Below is a framework to follow as we go through the chapter.

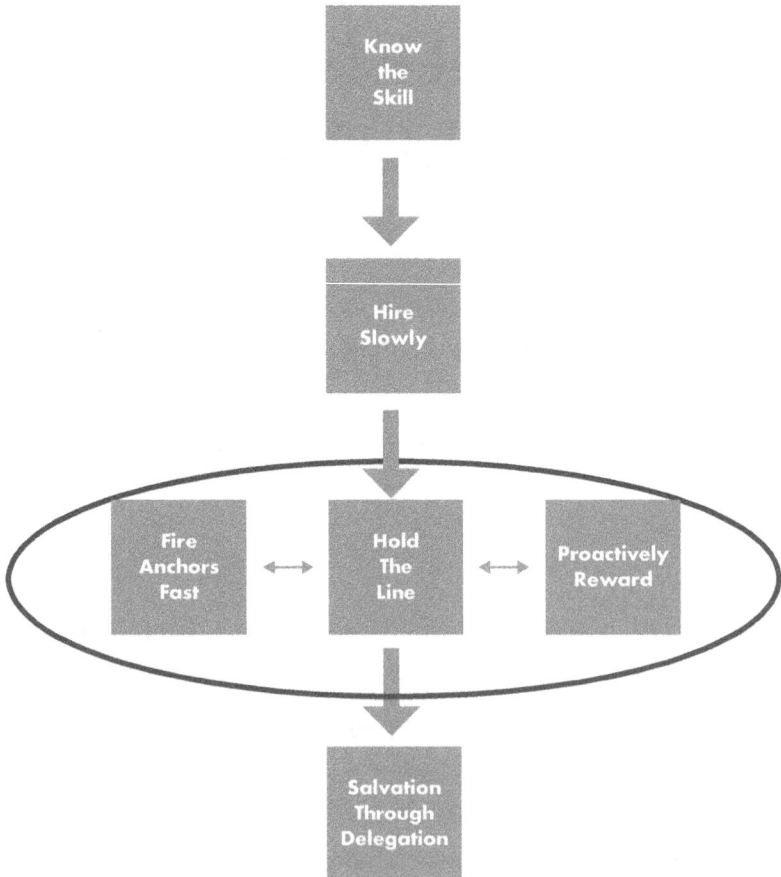

Know the Skill

It helps to be able to do the task you are hiring for. I was hiring an office manager for the industrial services company, and there had been robust demand through Craigslist and temp agencies. Hiring for an office job was a welcome break from the challenge of hiring CDLs and other field positions during the post-pandemic labor crunch. All the candidates had been "good," but I had yet to find the "great" one. Marylin walked in with a laminated résumé.

"I saw the posting online and wanted to stop by and drop off my résumé," she said.

"I like your style. There is no substitute for in-person," I responded.

This was going to be an in-person job, so the fact she came down was a great sign. I glanced through her résumé, and she seemed interview-worthy. She lived a few blocks away.

"Come back to my office for an interview," I said, gesturing to my office with an effusive positive energy.

"Oh, OK," she hesitantly agreed.

Marylin was getting an on-the-spot interview. It is always important to be prepared. Marylin had managed a doctor's office for over twenty years but decided to go to a non-profit after much soul-searching. Unfortunately, the non-profit had shut down during the pandemic. Now she was job searching. Our first conversation went well and was enough for a second interview. I invited her back the next day for an hour of shadowing me at 8:00 a.m. At this point, I was doing the office manager's job, so I had the golden opportunity to personally train the next office manager. Marylin showed up the next day at 7:45 a.m., signed the NDA, and watched me work for the next hour, asking all kinds of questions. After she left with her brain hurting, I called her old boss, who sang her praises and expressed sadness that Marylin no longer worked there.

I invited Marylin back for another few days of shadowing me. She showed up early every day sporting a smile, dressed professionally, and asked a ton of questions. Her dedication and excitement were apparent. Marylin lacked the hard skill set for the job, especially the quantitative skills required to work with accounts receivable (AR)/accounts payable (AP) and the technology experience outside of Microsoft that would define her day-to-day; however, what she lacked in skill she made up for with hunger and tenacity.

With six office visits, around ten hours of shadowing under our belt, and an interview with Tom, I was ready to give Marylin a shot. She would work through a temp agency for the first ninety days and then be hired as an employee with full benefits. A slow and methodical onboarding process maximizes appreciation for the position. The benefit of having an additional ninety days to evaluate Marylin's abilities was worth its weight in gold.

An investor, professor, and operator mentor of mine told me, "Nothing clarifies like clarity."

During her first ninety days, Marylin made clear she was going to get this job. She took becoming office manager as a challenge. She showed up at least fifteen minutes early every day—not 95 percent of days, but every day. By week two, she had brought homemade sliders for the field technicians to munch on and had rekindled the old practice of having candy available at her desk for them.

For a field service business, what happens in the office is of secondary importance to the work done out in the field. Part of Marylin's role was making sure the technicians did their jobs by analyzing their pictures and paperwork for nightmarish work, such as using a scraper and chemicals to clean grease from an exhaust system. To be given the privilege of sitting behind a desk and analyzing that type of work, an office employee needs to spend time in the field with the technicians.

Field days are a job requirement. I like a good surprise and want the experience to be genuine, so field days are always a surprise for the technicians. The office team member just shows up on-site out of the blue.

When I sent Marylin on her first field day during her evaluation period, the expectation was to observe, learn, and lend a helping hand if able. Marylin is in her mid-fifties and is of average physical health for her age. This particular job involved climbing a ladder to access a roof to clean a fan. I did not explicitly ask Marylin to go on the roof, nor did I explicitly tell her not to. In fact, I did not mention the roof at all. Upon returning from the job, Russell, the lead technician on the job, barged into my office with his usual Tasmanian Devil determination.

"Marylin is awesome," he said. "She actually helped on the job, and she was determined to join me on the roof to clean the fan. I encouraged her not to because of the rain, but she was insistent." He continued, "She gets after it!"

Impressing Russell is no easy feat. Marylin was crushing it.

Part of Marylin's job is managing AR, which requires balancing field service management AR with accounting AR during the weekly deposit. While this sounds easy, it is a monumental challenge. Marylin is required to work with hundreds of invoices across two databases that have only one-way communication, working on a task where there is zero margin for error (because the balances have to match up to the cent) and where a single misstep can lead to hours of catch-up work. This was a pure test of Marylin's tenacity.

Every Thursday, Marylin would take the challenge head-on and power forward to completion, which often required staying late. One particular Thursday was terrible; it had been a tough day from the beginning. Technician no-shows, emergency calls, and bad weather. To boot, the deposit did not balance. It was past 7:00 p.m., and the twelve-hour mark was behind her. Marylin had to go through every deposit line by line again. I checked her work, and it all balanced. A heartbreaker! It was a technical error on the part of the service provider. The time was around 8:30 p.m. I would be up the next day at 4:45 a.m. and Marylin not long thereafter. We called support and worked through the challenge. Mid-way through the call, when we were both depressed, drained, and distraught, Marylin dug deep, and we got it done, taking our relationship to a new level.

"Marylin, you have an uncanny ability to put your head down and work through things. You really grit it done," I said.

The following week, I was telling that story at an EO forum, and one of my mates recommended that I trademark the phrase. He even looked it up on the United States Trademark and Patent Office (USTPO) website. Sure enough, it was available, and Grit It Done was born.

Hire Slowly

One of my very best hires didn't come through a normal job posting and application process but organically through her immediate buy-in and enthusiasm for what we were doing.

I was sitting at the local coffee shop reviewing a spreadsheet outlining the tenant improvement budget for the prospective Anytime Fitness. I was plugging the latest quote from the carpet vendor into the proforma model when someone squeezed my bicep from the side. I glanced up and saw a woman who appeared to be in her fifties, bubbling with energy. She was looking down at me with an eager and excited gaze.

"Are you the one opening up the fitness club in town?" she asked.

"That's the plan. It is exciting times!" I shot back with passion. "There is a planning meeting on Tuesday where we hope to get the heads up."

"I'm Gina. I'll be at the meeting to support you, and I want to be the first member to sign up!" she said.

"Great. I'm Reid. It's a pleasure to meet you," I responded. My heart was smiling at the fact that a resident of the town was so excited. I was selling memberships already!

"You, too. See you on Tuesday," Gina said.

A pre-opening sale (presale) is a key step in opening a fitness center. Building a base of recurring monthly membership dues in advance means you will have predictable cash flow upon opening. This also provides cash in the bank (through, for example, an initiation fee) that can be used to pay pre-opening expenses, thereby minimizing the cash required to open. I chose to rent a classy mobile storage unit and furnish a temporary office in it.

Gina was out of town when the membership presale began. Reese, a man who, two weeks before, had stood up and unsuccessfully lobbied the planning commission to vote against the fitness center because of the dangerous precedent that a twenty-four-hour business would set, was the first to sign up with his sincerest apologies. When Gina got back from vacation, she came to the mobile storage unit as quickly as she could.

"Shoot! I was not the first member," she snapped with frustration. Recovering from her initial outburst, she enthusiastically signed up.

"Let me know if I can help in any way around the club," she said with an eager smile.

"Will do. I will reach out to you in a couple of weeks when we start the hiring process. In the meantime, each referral is good for $1 off your membership dues, so please keep them coming," I said, keeping my cards close to my chest.

At this point, I had a gut feeling that I had found my club manager. First, she understood small business; her husband owned the auto repair shop in town, and she had experienced a bumpy road operating a cruise booking business on her own. She understood that it was all fun and games as long as there were enough paying members. Second, she was a pillar of the community and viewed the fitness center as a means to continue her community involvement. Third, as an ex-body builder, she was into fitness. Fourth, she was fun, bubbly, outgoing, and enjoyable to be around. Gina had the goods.

It was early November, and the club was slated to open in mid-December. While having Gina start work immediately would have short-term value in increased presale memberships, I am a believer that a slower hiring process builds appreciation for the position, which leads to better performance and retention. In the words of my mentor Jason Payne, "Slow is smooth." My other fitness centers were fully staffed, so I was free to manage this club on my own until I had the right manager lined up. I was going to let Gina's enthusiasm build up like water behind a dam and see what kind of torrent she could unleash at the time of maximum demand, when the club was about to open.

Gina officially started the day after Christmas. I asked her to show up at 10:00 a.m. and to work until 7:00 p.m. For the first five days, she was there from at least 9:00 a.m. until 8:00 p.m. and even came in on Saturday. She sold dozens of memberships, soaked up every operational detail like a sponge, and made sure the club was spotless. *Cleanliness is next to godliness* is a saying I live by in every area of my life. During her helping-out period, Gina was already acting like the owner of the club. She was in her element building a community with her incessant levels of enthusiasm; she was lightning in a bottle. After her first week volunteering, Gina was rewarded with a free one-year membership, a bottle of nice champagne, a $100 bill, and a job offer to be club manager.

"I want you to hear the cha-ching sound of the cash register opening," Gina said after accepting the offer.

"Let's motivate the community to get active!" I couldn't wait to get started together.

"Yeah!" Gina responded as we high fived and ended with a happy hug.

Gina and I were off to the races. The relationship that started with a bicep squeeze at a coffee shop turned into a rewarding, long-term friendship.

Fire Anchors Fast

Hiring slowly and firing quickly is the key to retaining entrepreneurial employees. One bad apple can affect the entire batch.

Dane was a good employee. In February 2020, he was going to move an hour away from the shop, making commuting difficult. He told us he was going to transition out; he chose to no-show. He was fired for cause, per the employee handbook. After being fired, he applied for unemployment. If we allowed him to get unemployment, even though he was fired for cause, we would be enabling dishonesty. It would increase our and his previous employer's unemployment insurance rate and would increase system-wide costs that are ultimately borne by taxpayers. I appealed. I had to send in copies of the relevant employee handbook clauses, the write-ups, screenshots of text messages, and the schedule, among other documents. I sent in over forty pages of documents and invested hours of work. He lost. He again appealed. I had to send in additional documents and then go through a hearing that was scheduled and mutually agreed to. Our side showed; Dane did not. It got rescheduled because he claimed a hardship excuse. We showed up again for the second hearing. The judge reviewed the facts, and we won. Anchors weigh down the organization, and company culture is strengthened when they are held accountable.

Proactively Reward

Entrepreneurial employees never have to ask me for a raise. I proactively reward them and never give them a reason to go elsewhere. I understand the value they add to business and my life. After working for me for two years, I gave Gina 10 percent profit sharing, and each year I raised Tom's base pay at 2x the rate of inflation. There are plenty of times as an EBO where it is smart to live by the saying, *A penny saved is a penny earned.* When it comes to investing in entrepreneurial employees, though, the philosophy is, "Go big or go home." While money is an important component, understanding your employees' intrinsic motivation and managing to that end is the key. Letting entrepreneurial employees do more is often the solution.

Thrive Through Delegation

Solicitors of all kinds constantly came by the fitness club in suburban Sacramento. People were looking for jobs, hawking credit card terminals, selling specialty carpet cleaners, asking for money, and doing missionary work; I have seen it all. Bobby Boyd came by during the presale, offering his services as a massage therapist in partnership with the club. Other massage therapist solicitors had come by the club. I had passed on every opportunity because my focus was on membership sales. What stood out about Bobby was that sporting a healthy gut and a sales centric attitude, this was the last person I would ever want to get a massage from. My first reaction was that this man needed a career change. That opinion became cemented when I learned that his background was in construction preceded by sales.

"I have sold alarm systems and golf clubs over the phone. I can sell anything to anyone," Bobby declared with resolve. "Who is selling your memberships here?"

We were off to the races. After our initial on-the-spot interview, I followed up with his references and learned that this guy really could sell. I invited him down to the club again and had him sell me from start to finish. I challenged him with every roadblock in the book. Dumb questions, interruptions, a partner objecting, and accusations of pressure. The process lasted over an hour. Bobby was good.

After digesting the sales experience, I invited him down again. The club was a ten-minute walk from his house. A convenient commute is a meaningful plus. I painted the vision of a sales job leading to a club manager role for this single club with "potentially" more responsibility as we opened more clubs. It is easy to sell a salesman. The next day, he accepted the offer with a Monday start date. It was spring 2008, and the financial crisis was in full swing. Unemployment in the area was approaching 10 percent, and the foreclosure signs were coming in droves. No money, no house, no problem. Nothing was going to stop Bobby Boyd from selling.

Once Bobby (with the help of Captain Running Man) got the club cash flow positive, he was promoted as promised. Bobby wanted me to leave him alone to manage the club and open more clubs so that I could grow the pie for everyone. His attitude toward me was, "Hit the road, Jack. I got this." Bobby allowed me to thrive through delegation. This gave me the freedom I needed to actively grow the business.

The Four Ps

The entrepreneurial employees I invested in at my businesses went on to generate meaningful financial returns and, more importantly, I enjoyed my time with them. I analyzed thirty-two financially successful business sales, and relationships with entrepreneurial employees are a critical factor in seller fulfillment and business success. In addition, they are often viable candidates to buy the business. Here are four factors that entrepreneurial employees have in common:

Punctuality

They show up early, come ready to work, and stay late without having to be asked. The buck stops with them. If something needs to be done by a certain time, they don't complain; they just do it.

Profit drive

Purpose, mission, and intrinsic motivation matter to all good employees. What differentiates an entrepreneurial employee is their desire for the owner to make lots of money and prosper. They understand that, social good aside, the business needs to pay the bills and generate a healthy profit. They act with an innate eye to the bottom line. I have never had to teach entrepreneurial employees about profit and loss; they inherently get that higher prices, more volume, and fewer costs create profit. Entrepreneurial employees actively pursue the profit agenda out of a desire to contribute. Bobby sold memberships so that I could make enough money to be able to open more clubs; Gina wanted me to be able to afford an engagement ring; Tom wanted me to pay down the business debt so I could have financial freedom; and Marylin simply said, "My business is to make you money." Entrepreneurial employees understand that good things come their way when the profits are rolling in. I always increased their compensation based on strong performance.

Passion

Entrepreneurial employees have their own special ways of showing passion. Bobby's frustration with other team members' inability to perform has given him migraines. Gina's concern about letting me or the community down by underperforming (typically in an immaterial way) sometimes brought her to tears. Tom's passion of choice was profanity-laden rampages about operations not being perfect and people being incompetent. Marylin constantly lost sleep over open loops, such as a customer issue left unresolved or an emergency call missed. Entrepreneurial employees care, and their emotions show it. I embrace the outbursts.

Persistently innovative

Entrepreneurial employees innovate ways to make the EBO's life easier. They solve problems, often without talking about them. While it is an art to know when to ask for help, entrepreneurial employees take the monkeys off the EBO's back to the point that the EBO does not know they exist. Take an example of a customer complaint. As opposed to telling me about it, Tom would call the customer, talk with the technician, and arrange a solution with me being none the wiser. Problem arises, problem solved. There is no need for me to know.

If blessed with the presence of an entrepreneurial employee, fight hard to keep them around. A monumental reason for EBO success is the presence of entrepreneurial employees. Dennis is a successful private equity investor and mentor of mine who has provided life-changing liquidity to dozens of EBOs. He often reminds me, "Every successful business has a Gina."

The Definition of Dedication

Dancing Dan is a sign spinner. I had seen him promoting businesses in areas around the fitness clubs. Most sign spinners I saw exuded an "I do not want to be doing this" attitude, spinning the sign with limited enthusiasm or barely spinning it at all. Dancing Dan was in a constant state of movement and spirit as he spun with unrivaled energy, dressed up as either Spider-Man, Superman, or Iron Man. A true community superhero!

Dan looked to be in his mid-fifties and was in killer physical shape. He spoke with a drawl and would ride his bike in any weather to the club, showing up at least an hour early. He would then lift weights for around thirty minutes before embarking on his day of spinning. He would spin from 7:00 a.m. until around 5:00 p.m. When I purchased a sign to be spun, I took it out for a test spin. I am in excellent physical shape. Mimicking Dancing Dan was easy for around two minutes. My form started to suffer around minute seven, and by minute twelve, I could no longer feel my lats or medial deltoids. Almost every day, often seven days a week, Dan was out there doing his thing for approximately eight hours. He reliably clocked in around 150 pounds, with between 4.2 and 4.4 percent body fat.

Dan had kids and a significant other. He was intellectually disabled and could have relied on the benevolence of others, yet he figured out a way to support his family, bring a smile to the community, and add value to the economy day in and day out. I tried to figure out how Dancing Dan came to be and who had helped him along the way. I have immense respect for that person or group of people. Perhaps he did it all on his own.

I am honored to have worked with him for the years I was actively involved in the club. Dancing Dan does not make excuses; he shows up early and gets it done. It inspires me. On the days I am tired, do not want to push forward, and want to be lazy, I ask myself what Dancing Dan would do, and I step up accordingly. When team members who are facing their own life challenges manufacture excuses about how hard the work is, I think back to Dancing Dan. It reminds me that there are two kinds of workers: those who find a way and those who find an excuse. Dancing Dan finds a way.

Good, Better, Best

It is my duty to push my team members to level up their lives. At the industrial services business, one of my employees, Terry, believed in the power of self-improvement. The combination of self-improvement and self-interest is a potent motivator of behavior change. Terry was not receiving his COVID-19 stimulus checks because he was not filing his taxes. Three years before, he had received a letter from the IRS about falsely claiming a dependent. His knee-jerk reaction was, "Never mind the IRS," and he decided to stop filing and paying taxes.

"It was a bad decision," he said when he came to me asking for guidance.

I took on this project for three reasons. 1) I am motivated to help team members be better citizens; 2) I believe that most people will go above and beyond for me if I go above and beyond for them; and 3) I enjoy learning about how the plumbing of our country works and how challenging it can be to navigate.

Having always filed my taxes on time, I was not sure where to begin with a tardy tax payment. Online tax software could do the trick. I worked with Terry on getting the necessary information, which was a heavy lift. I filled in the tax forms for him and made sure he was providing me with the right data. He was going to sign the documents and, once filed, he would owe over $10,000—quite a chunk of change for his wage range.

At the end of 2020, Terry's taxes were finally ready to go. The plan was to file and then, when the bills came, to file an offer-in-compromise (OIC) with the IRS to get the balance eliminated, which I thought we had a 50-50 chance of achieving. The IRS was quick to send Terry his stimulus checks. Money talks! Terry was happy as a clam. The IRS, however, took months, then more months, to respond to the OIC. They promised deadlines and then missed them. I spent hours on hold with them. Eventually, they responded, and the agent rejected the OIC. Terry owed in full. He stepped up and decided he was going to get on a payment plan to pay in full. I am proud of Terry for embarking on this journey.

The key takeaway is that an ounce of prevention is worth a pound of cure. While Terry could have prevented this by paying on time, it is never too late to do the right thing.

After I sold the business, Terry sent me the following email:

> "Hey Reid! Hope all is well with you and family. I wanted to say thank you for pushing me and making me a better person. Wanted to let you know I took your advice and got a secured CC from Discover. I actually got my down payment back and have a 1,000 credit limit. Plz keep in touch and hope life is treating you well. If you have any more advice, let me know."

The most fulfilling part about entrepreneurial business ownership is improving lives. Even though we lost the OIC, I am glad to see that the push paid off and Terry is continuing to live by the mantra, *Good, better, best.*

Action Item

Visit www.reidtileston.com/grititdone to tell us about an entrepreneurial employee you know and love.

CHAPTER 7

USE PEER GROUPS

Peer groups empower. Most people think you can join a peer group once you are success-ful; in reality, you join a peer group to become successful.

Lonely Owner Syndrome is a term that CEO Zane Carol first told me before I was an EBO in 2007. Zane was a private equity associate at the time, responsible for sourcing deals. He talked to business owners nonstop. They often did not have many people who understood what the life of a business owner was like. Spouses, friends, advisors, and employees are good for certain conversations, but there are some is-sues only other EBOs understand and, in the absence of a peer group to talk to, loneliness at the top ensues. In this chapter, we will discuss the importance of finding a peer group.

As a franchisor, Anytime Fitness helped with this by encouraging dialogue among club owners. A network of other club owners who get it is valuable. The more contact and collaboration their owners have, the better. While networking with other franchisees is critical, big-time value comes from doing the work with operators outside your industry in a formal forum setting.

Having a network of club owners was not enough for me. I had my Anytime Fitness clubs around the California central valley, running themselves and making good money. I was bored. I caught Lonely Owner Syndrome. Opening new clubs did not excite me anymore. With hindsight, I can see that my loneliness drove me to spend $120,000 in business school tuition and dedicate my full-time efforts to school. If I had done the vulnerability work offered by peer groups pre-business school, my life may have turned out differently.

I learned my lesson. In future endeavors, I was hungry to get involved in an operator group. I knew from the fitness clubs how critical this aspect would be to improving operations. In spring 2020, as the pandemic was in full swing, a lot of business owners were thinking about survival while I was thinking about preventing a second bout of Lonely Owner Syndrome. Due to the pandemic, Entrepreneurs' Organization (EO) was losing members and struggling to get new ones. I was excited to join, and I am convinced that I was their easiest sale of 2020. EO is really not about solving business problems; it is about you and how you show up in your business. I aspired to have a forum where I could share my business owner problems with a group of peers whose shoulders I could cry on. Doing vulnerability work during our monthly forum is valuable. The key is doing the right kind of vulnerability work with the right people.

Peer Groups Empower

Being an EBO can be a lonely journey if you let it be. From the moment you consider the EBO path, you should engage with a peer group. They can provide support and accountability and share experiences that will prove invaluable to you as you explore your opportunities. I am a proponent of Promise Partners, a business ownership incubator in Cleveland that has led sixty-five individuals down the path of business ownership. As Sam Ludwig from Promise Partners says, "I can speak for myself and most Promise Partners members that navigating this path would not have been successful without the peer support and mentorship Promise provided. For many months prior to launching my search, I received encouragement, accountability, and specific ideas on how best to attract investors, position myself as a highly credible buyer, and many other insights related to key aspects of the journey that led to the success of my first acquisition."

While I was not a member of Promise Partners before I was a business owner, I strongly recommend joining a similar group as you embark on your EBO journey.

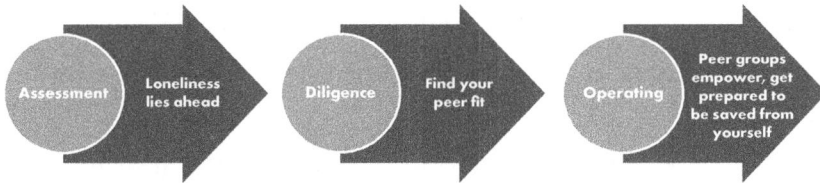

Let's go through a few examples to illustrate the power of peer groups.

How Peer Groups Help Overcome Employee Challenges
Peer groups operate as a reality check and are instrumental in helping EBOs navigate tricky challenges. Over sixteen years, I have learned that most challenges are people-centric and emotionally charged, which prevent an EBO from seeing things clearly on their own. I am

going to tell you a story that illustrates the power of peer groups for an EBO and how a peer group helped me through it.

Tom was key to the past, present, and future of the industrial services business I owned. His son, Taylor, was the leader-in-waiting. Tom and I were preparing him. When I bought the business, however, Taylor's driver's license had been suspended due to an Operating While Intoxicated violation. Taylor was handy and intuitively knew the business. He also brought new skills to the table. He had a calming presence, was an excellent teacher, and had a grit-it-done attitude, all while sporting the necessary field skills. He was the natural leader and critical to my long-term vision for the business.

I saw Taylor's potential and pushed him to step up. A few months after buying the business, I focused on helping Taylor get his license back. I lent him the money and created a personal relationship with his treatment professionals to help shepherd the process forward. If Taylor got off-track, missed an appointment, or was not making the necessary progress, I would be in the loop. I also promised him a raise when he got his license. Money talks! Taylor saw the process through. It was a glorious day of celebration when he could drive on his own once again.

With his driver's license in hand, next up was his commercial driver's license (CDL). As a recently licensed CDL myself, I could help teach. Taylor had already been moving the trucks around the shop for years and was a naturally excellent driver.

As with his driver's license, Taylor would get a nice pay bump with the CDL. I spend freely when it comes to people's development. After a month of training, Taylor was ready to take the CDL examination.

Enter Mean Tester Mark! The first test was set for a Saturday morning, so it did not interfere with revenue generation. It was a cold

January day when we met Mark in a parking lot. I dropped Taylor off and then walked to a Starbucks. Taylor failed.

Despite this setback, Taylor powered forward. He is not a quitter and knows failure is one building block of success. Fast forward two weeks, and Taylor had his CDL. With his CDL in hand, he was like a kid in a candy shop. He took ownership of his truck. He treated it like it was his baby. It was clean, organized, and seemed to run better. He upped his game, making the other driver who used the truck act out with bouts of insecure envy because there was a better operator in town. Taylor was becoming a leader. I did not keep this to myself. I consistently told him that he had a bright future and great things would continue to come his way. My actions spoke louder than words. A year later, he asked me for help when he was considering getting his own place. I was more than happy to assist. I am excited to help people push their lives forward. He did excellent work for me, and I wanted his life to get better.

Accept Reality

On a Friday afternoon, Taylor told me he had started a side hustle courier business. I was speechless. Fridays are consistently the worst day of the week, and Friday afternoon is consistently the worst time of the day. A maelstrom of emergency calls, employee no-shows, frustrated customers, and news like I had received from Taylor seem to have a strange attraction to Friday.

"OK," I said after a few painfully awkward seconds as I worked to digest what was happening. At this point, I had been knocked around with bad surprises so many times that more of the same felt reassuringly comfortable. "Are you planning to continue to work here?" I asked as I slowly regained my voice.

"Yes. I just wanted to be straightforward with you. It is mostly my girlfriend doing the driving," he responded. "Sorry to drop this on you."

"Thank you for telling me," I answered. "I will digest this and follow up if further discussion is warranted." I wished him a good weekend.

I did my best to keep a strong appearance, while deep down I was deflated and distressed. Tom came in afterward to tell me he found out a few weeks ago and had encouraged Taylor to tell me as quickly as possible.

"He's not going anywhere," Tom quickly said.

On Monday, I met Taylor at the conclusion of a job, got in a truck with him, and drove us to the next job. Nothing clarifies like clarity. I was feeling certain that Taylor was a man of his word, but I figured I would ask directly.

"Taylor, what I heard from you on Friday is that you have a side hustle and that it is not going to interfere with this work. Is that correct?" I asked.

"Yes," he said, confidently.

"OK. If that changes at any point, are you going to let me know?" I inquired.

"Yep, boss. I am all-in," he responded.

"Great."

We were waiting for a train to pass, and Taylor started talking about how his son liked trains. It seemed like we were back to our old comfortable ways. At this point in my career, nothing really surprised me. I had grown thick skin over the years.

Little did I know this would turn out to be Taylor's last day.

Surprise is an understatement. The following day, he went completely off the grid. At first, we thought something was wrong. He was not returning anyone's calls. Rinse and repeat on Wednesday.

Taylor had recently moved and had never officially given me his new address. It took me ten minutes of internet research to figure it out. I was worried, so the next day I drove down to what I thought was his house. A young kid answered the door.

"Is Taylor OK?" I asked.

His silence, coupled with the van around the back, confirmed for me that I had found the right address, and his facial expression gave away the fact that Taylor was OK.

"He's not around," he finally said.

"Tell him we are all concerned about him," I said.

"Sure," he replied.

I thanked him and left. At the time, we were completing an emergency job, and the team came together to cover for Taylor and grit it done. Taylor showed up the next week, and we formalized his exit.

Be Pragmatic

The sale of the business was moving forward. We had a signed letter of intent, and the new buyer was deep into diligence. The CEO and head of expansion were visiting me on the second day of Taylor's no-showing. The on-paper solution was simple: I would lead by example, get in the field, and do customer jobs as needed while I hired and trained another CDL. The path ahead was manageable in theory.

I had invested a lot in Taylor over the years, and it took time for me to let go.

My advisers and peers observed me try to scuttle the deal over Taylor. Alex Fall and Chris Simmons were both members of EO.

"I think that this matters a lot more to you than it does to the buyer," Alex said.

"I had a person do me wrong, and it left me bedridden for a year and a half. People suck," Chris added.

"Just grit it done, hire a new CDL, and get on with it," Alex chimed in.

They told me exactly what I needed to hear. My advisers got me out of my own head. The conversation with the buyer was simple. Taylor no-showed, his co-workers and I are stepping up, and I am hiring a new CDL. No problems in life, only solutions. My peer group saved me from myself.

Now it was time to execute. Ruthless has a name; it is Miguel. After a painful recruiting process in which dozens upon dozens of candidates did not make the cut, he was on track every step of the way. Ruthless was a shining star. He was a golden boy from the beginning. To Ruthless, in the field there are no problems, only solutions. If a manhole cover will not open, it is only because he has not hit it with a sledgehammer hard enough! Ruthless has a grit-it-done attitude and turned out to be a great replacement for Taylor.

How to Take Timely Advice

Alex is scatter-brained. He is easily distracted and goes off on tangents like they are his best friend. I am focused, disciplined, and intentional with my comments. I live and breathe Occam's Razor; less is more. Opposites must attract. Alex knows how to give advice when it counts. One day, I was under significant stress while trying to sell a business.

Employee drug tests and criminal records were top of my mind. When required for compliance or if there is suspicion that a team member is coming to work under any form of influence, I will drug test. Aside from that, my policy is to not test. The buyer, however, required all team members to pass a drug and background check for "insurance reasons." I was not confident that every team member would pass a drug test. I had a dilemma: I was not going to take a chance on an employee not passing and the buyer walking away, but I also did not want to scare the buyer away by refusing to test. Alex reminded me to think about the person on the other side of the table.

"Think about how bad it will be for the guy on their side if the deal gets blown," he stated with his signature smile. "You are not the only one under pressure."

This gentle reminder packed a lot of punch, as the pressure was mounting. Alex had bought and sold a number of businesses; he understood the anguish I was going through. The buyer and I came to a reasonable agreement that non-commercial drivers would be given sixty days post-close to pass a drug test, and the buyer would review the background checks before employee conversations. No problems in life, only solutions.

Alex was not the only one in my corner. Rich was a member of an operator mastermind. Rich knows how to sell, which means he gets people and knows how to have crucial conversations. The buyer had a two-week window, between which the employees were going to be told about the sale and the deal was going to close. A key part of the deal for me was providing retention bonuses to the team, as their leaving could threaten the deal. They did not know that, though. I had the delicate job of finding a way to communicate that a deal was happening, that their jobs were secure, and that they would be getting a retention bonus because this buyer and I saw eye to eye.

Rich and I role-played the conversations with the team members. Rich allowed me to get out of my own way. My pre-Rich conversation would have gone like this: "I am selling the business. You will meet the buyer tomorrow; the deal is going to close in two weeks, and you will be getting a retention bonus with 25 percent paid out in a quarter and 75 percent in one year." Transparent, honest, and transactional—the Reid Tileston style.

When I presented this approach to Rich, I felt him cringe. It took him forty-five minutes of consulting with an amateur like me to word-smith my delivery to where it needed to be. In this context, the Reid Tileston style needed improvement. His mastery is outlined below with my reflections in parentheses in italics:

"I am selling the business (*you cannot stop it*). The new buyer and I see eye to eye on the importance of the current team members, and because of this, you will be getting a retention bonus (*This buyer does, but other buyers may not, so do not try to get cute and ask for more*). The new buyer will be here tomorrow at 8:00 a.m., and I will be around for the transition."

The conversations all went well. Thank you, Rich, for getting me from a six to a ten!

In the months leading up to the sale, I had a dozen peer business operators available to me 24/7 to provide practical advice and emotional support as I worked to get the deal over the finish line. These EBOs and CEOs had experience successfully acquiring companies, selling to strategic buyers, watching deals fall apart at the finish line, and everything in between. The group sported industry experience across the board in education, healthcare, manufacturing, tech, consumer services, and logistics. Their experience ran the gamut. The best part was all these individuals knew me. They knew my life, what made me tick, my strengths, my weaknesses, and my aspirations. We had been doing confidential monthly check-ins where we discussed the real issues of business and life—that is, the issues that I did not want to confront and could not talk to anyone else about. Then the group would take those issues and go deep on them. The crew knew my deep dark secrets. And I did not have just one of these groups, I had two: Entrepreneurs Organization and a Graduate School Mastermind Operator Group. The value of these groups was immeasurable.

Peer Group Cost/Benefit

The cost of EO is approximately $5,000 per year, and the cost of the Operator Group is zero—meals and retreats aside. The operator group was an outcropping of business school, so an argument could be made that it would not be available if I had not paid my tuition. The value these groups provide to the members who go all-in is immeasurable. Consultants, lawyers, accountants, and other service providers generally give content expertise and transactional services; those have their place. But operator groups provide their own experience and share the experiences of others. Operator groups also provide the "container" in which to grow personal relationships. Fellow operators are the best strategic advisors at the best price, and the relationships that develop are truly priceless. As you research peer groups and seek to grow your network, explore the robust Small Medium Business (SMB) community on Twitter and searchfunder.com

Be Thoughtful in Choosing Your Strategic Advisers

When managing transactional strategic advisers, judge them on their attention to detail and their response time. Peer groups are valuable strategic advisers that can provide important guidance at critical times while also helping combat Lonely Owner Syndrome. A strategic adviser is often assumed to be a service provider, such as an attorney or accountant. I have worked with a few service providers who were true strategic advisers. Many of the other paid advisors I have had were transactional, while my peer groups were truly transformational.

When it comes to legal and accounting, the devil is in the details. I have witnessed highly paid professionals, leaders in their fields, miss material clauses that turned out to be costly for EBOs. I have personally had the opportunity to sign documents that had mistakes in my favor. A sophisticated EBO turned investor (for whom I have a lot of respect) once signed a document that gave an equity holder hundreds of thousands in additional value because of a few unfortunate words around how the number was calculated. His attorney drafted and reviewed the document. I have also seen attorneys derail deals because they were slow to respond during the critical phase of negotiating sales documents. Time kills deals!

I often retreat to the do-it-yourself model of reviewing critical documents when the stakes are high. I expect to be held accountable for the documents I sign, so it is on me to understand them. Tragically, unnecessary complexity is often added to these documents, at times by bad actors for nefarious reasons. My invitation to the readers of this book is, for the good of the country, strive to keep it simple.

Private Equity

I have been in the orbit of private equity since early in my career. Private equity is an investment group that buys and sells small private businesses. Private equity is full of ripe acquisition ideas, so networking with private equity professionals is a smart practice. There is a vibrant debate around whether private equity is a good or bad thing for the country. What is not in doubt, however, is that private equity professionals are a wealth of information for prospective and current EBOs. Effective EBOs ask questions and learn. It is truly win-win. My only advice is to realize that you are swimming with sharks. Have an ironclad NDA before you disclose anything that remotely matters to you. You have heard me say it a number of times now, but it's especially true in this case: those with the gold make the rules. Private equity controls a lot of gold. The most recent study I read is that private equity firms had $3.4 trillion globally in dry powder (money available to invest in acquisitions).[25]

25 | bain.com/insights/private-equity-market-in-2021-global- private-equity-report-2022/#:~:text=After%2010%20years%20of%20steady,see%20Figures%208%20and%20 9)

Action Item

Visit www.reidtileston.com/grititdone and tell us about a group you joined at any point in your life that brought out your ideal self.

CHAPTER 8

VISUALIZE
YOUR EXIT

Work hard now to get rewarded later. Most people think that buyers find you. In reality, EBOs research potential acquirers before they buy.

Achieving an exit is one worthy goal for an EBO. In this chapter, I'll teach you the Position for Sale framework, which provides a method for maximizing value for acquirers—especially those with deep pockets, such as strategic buyers (think of them as competitors or companies that have synergies) and private equity investors.

Position For Sale Framework

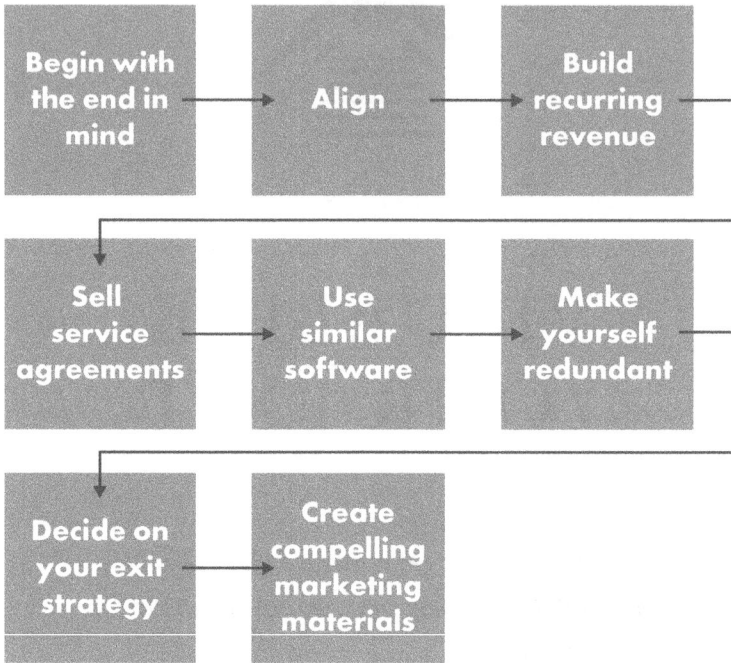

Begin with the End in Mind

Think carefully through who potential acquirers are during the re-search phase. When selling the industrial services business, I knew there were strategic acquirers in the industry. During diligence, I asked a friend to call them and ask what they thought about my acqui-sition target. With this information, I knew how to strategically focus the business, as well as how to get a sense of valuation. When it comes time to sell, intermediaries, accountants, and/or valuation firms can be paid to put together opinions of value. Often, intermediaries will do it for free. Ultimately, these evaluations are only opinions; the real value is what the business ends up selling for.

Align Your Strategy to Your Acquirer

Once you have the avatar of your potential acquirer and an idea of how much they might pay, align your strategy to maximize the attractiveness of your business. You never know when an unsolicited offer might come, so you are best served to make your business as attractive as possible at all times. For the industrial services company, the acquirers with the deepest pockets were pumping companies, so I prioritized pumping over the other service lines to make myself a more attractive target. Bryce is the CEO of a roofing company that offered a mix of residential and commercial services who identified a commercial acquirer as being able to pay the most, so he focused his efforts on growing the commercial roofing business.

Revenue

To summarize what was discussed in Chapter 3, recurring revenue is gold and repeating revenue is silver. Chapter 3 outlined why this is important for an inexperienced operator. Acquirers value it for the same reasons you valued it during your search.

Service Agreements

Recurring and repeating revenue is good. Recurring and repeating revenue coupled with service agreements is better. Recurring revenue coupled with a service agreement is best. Recurring service agreements mitigate risk, so it is important to create recurring services and sell recurring service agreements. Migrating to recurring service agreements has been a significant value driver for several EBO acquisitions. An EBO of a landscaping company significantly increased the value of his exit by moving from on-demand, informal agreements to recurring service agreements.

Similar Software

Integrating differing software can be a challenge, so changing your business' systems to match potential acquirers' will increase the attractiveness of your business. When deciding on which systems to use, I asked representatives from potential acquirers at a trade show which software they used. I learned that a viable acquirer was using one platform and was in the process of switching to another. I chose the one that they were switching to and increased the attractiveness of the business to them. They were the ones that eventually bought the business.

Make Yourself Redundant

As an EBO, you want to make yourself as redundant as possible to the business operations. Your responsibility is to be as general as possible so your business will fit into the acquirer's structure. In the case of the industrial services business, when fully staffed with CDLs, the business ran itself, and I was free to pursue owner activities such as HR, strategic finance, and technology strategy—the same roles the strategic acquirers had the built-in infrastructure for. I made it the perfect bolt-on acquisition for a platform company.

Decide on Your Exit Strategy

There are a number of exit options available. Sell to a competitor, sell to an employee, sell to a strategic acquirer (such as a competitor, supplier or customer), sell to a private equity firm, pass it on to your children, do an Employee Stock Ownership Plan (ESOP), or sell to an EBO. Deciding who to sell to and how to structure the transaction is significant, both financially and emotionally.

When deciding how to sell the industrial services business, I narrowed it down to two options: make the company an ESOP or sell to a strategic buyer. An ESOP is an employee benefit plan that enables all employees (from truck drivers to the executive assistant) to own part or all of the company they work for.

My heart wanted the team to enjoy the benefits of ownership because they were the ones doing the grueling field work. I went through the process of getting an ESOP transaction underwritten with an SBA 7a loan and approved through an SBA lender credit committee—a task I liken to climbing Mt. Everest immediately followed by K-2. ESOPs are made enormously complex by regulations, which make them difficult for small business owners to navigate without paying hefty fees. The ESOP upside was tremendous. Even though the loan interest rate was 175 basis points higher than the SBA 7a loan I used to purchase the business three years earlier and the loan was bigger, cash flow to the business would have improved because both the interest and the principal are tax deductible. If you hate taxes, you will love ESOPs. The tax benefits to sellers are lucrative, while to the companies, they are a competitive advantage that can fuel growth.

The structure was set up so that employees would have had their ownership tied up for ten years (the life of the SBA 7a loan) due to the ESOP exception. The business would not have to deal with a liquidity challenge for a decade due to employee withdrawals. Setting up an ESOP would have significantly improved cash flow even though it would have required additional hard compliance costs, such as a board and annual valuation. The ESOP exit would have put more money in my pocket than the highest opinions of value I received from the intermediaries.

In the end, I chose not to pull the trigger because an ESOP would have slowed decision-making, leading to lost agility, which is a competitive advantage. I reached out to a strategic buyer and asked for a price that would make me as well-off as the ESOP would have and left ample money to pay the team members sizable retention bonuses. My heart wanted to do employee ownership, but I concluded that cash would be more valuable to the team members.

In early conversations with the strategic buyer, it was important to establish that they were on board to pay retention bonuses; if you give a team member meaningful money, they may retire or use the money to go out and buy their own truck. The buyer was on board with the amounts and the timing. It was of paramount importance to me that the team members were taken care of as part of the transaction. Between the improved healthcare benefits, the more comprehensive ancillary benefit offerings, the cash bonuses, the resources of a larger company, and the prospect of moving up with a growing company, I reasoned it was the right move. As an EBO, you always want to leave the business better than you found it. I do have the occasional feel-bad moment that they have to deal with the red tape of a larger company, but in the grander scheme of things, I believe it is a small price to pay. With that said, I kept the ESOP as a viable alternative in my back pocket all the way through the closing process.

Create Compelling Marketing Materials

Avoid being the diamond in the rough. When it comes to marketing your business, invest the time and money to make sure the wrapping is as good as the gift itself. Whether you engage an intermediary or sell on your own using your strategic advisors and peer group as support, gather the data and make it look pretty and professional. Put together effective marketing materials such as a confidential information memorandum (CIM), which gives an overview of the business. While a good CIM will answer most questions, you must know the document well so that you can answer tough questions on the fly when asked

during the sales process. Doing this project will also help you understand how valuable your business really is.

Action Item

Visit www.reidtileston.com/grititdone to tell us
about a time that you effectively used visualization
to help you achieve a goal.

CHAPTER 9

HOW TO CLOSE

Buckle up! Most people think that selling a successful business should be easy; in reality, closing a transaction is a monumental task with a myriad of issues that can make for a wild ride.

Once you prepare your company to sell with these steps, it's time to apply your Grit It Done mindset to the art of closing the deal. The previous steps all lead here. Actions speak louder than words, and the ability to grit it done brings it all together. There are two kinds of individuals: those who grit it done and those who find excuses. EBOs grit it done. The following story will illustrate the Grit It Done decision framework in the context of selling the industrial services business.

Assessment: the Diligence Checklist
The law firm hired by the buyer sent a forty-three-page diligence

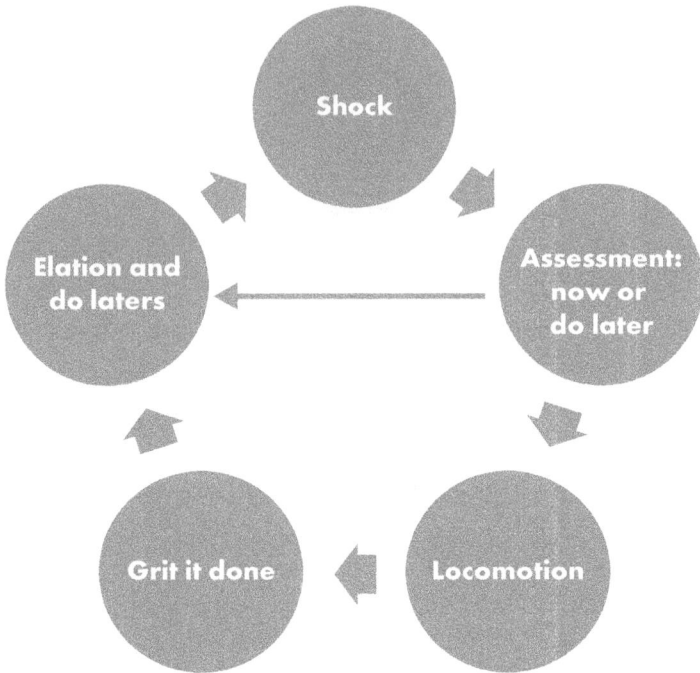

checklist to me at 3:00 p.m. on a weekday. I glanced at it for ten minutes. The list was so thorough and represented such a monumental task that it almost made me puke. I was in shock at the ask! I took a deep breath and dove into assessment. The good news was that half of it did not apply to me. The bad news was that it was still going to take an intense six hours to complete. Delays in completion would slow down the deal.

Because it was a legal document, I had two options:

1) I could pay my attorney to fill it out. That would entail him reviewing it, asking me about everything, having me provide everything, having their legal team tell my attorney that something was missing, and then having that relayed back to me. What a quagmire!

2) Do it myself.

It was a no-brainer. I resolved then and there that I was going to finish the entire list that night. I moved into locomotion (taking action) and in the cracks between tending to my daily tasks and the usual issues that arose, I put a few hours into it from the office. Later that evening, I picked up the work from my apartment, and I scratched and clawed it to completion. It was painstaking work, requiring me to reference numerous documents across a variety of databases. Of course, I had to do not one but two happenstance "password resets" on an already painful night. Those are the worst! Nevertheless, I powered forward and got it done shortly past midnight. I felt proud as I uploaded it to the legal section of the online diligence folder. I took even more pride when I emailed the sender to inform them it was taken care of. I was on a mission to close this deal as quickly as possible. I was shocked by the ask, assessed it, decided to do it straight away, cranked it to completion, and was able to be present for the tasks that lay ahead in the morning.

Unfortunately, my elation was short-lived. My blood boiled a few weeks later when my attorney emailed me to inform me that the buyer had again asked for the forty-three-page diligence checklist, which was holding things up. Within minutes, I forwarded them the email along with a link to the folder. They had sent the document; I had hurried to fill it out, and they did not even know that it had been received. I love having time-dated documents as a reminder. Once I got past my frustration, I used this as motivation to push even harder.

Focusing and being present are critical to peak performance. Open loops are a killer. Decide to do it now or be content that it can be done later. Both gritting it done in the present and intentionally deciding to do it later are steps forward because they eliminate the mental weight of indecision.

Be Prepared: the CEO Call

Bill (the head of expansion for the buyer), Josh (the CEO), and I jumped on a Zoom call to discuss the business. I was prepared and nervous. This was my first interaction with Josh. I readied myself with the music video for Bon Jovi's "It's My Life" on the Crush Tour in Switzerland. When Josh logged on, I thought his office looked like a cross between a college library and a lawyer's office. Mahogany chairs with green leather and books—lots of books. Josh was going to be like a sapper looking for land mines as he sought to uncover the risks of buying the business.

The CIM I had sent them was thorough. The buyer was a grease-trap pumping company. Pumping was their sweet spot. The rest of what we did presented a potential headache.

"What kind of work do you do at at your biggest factory customers?" Josh asked.

"Mainly cleaning exhaust systems," I replied with a less-is-more attitude.

"What does that entail?" he asked, trying to gauge the level of complexity.

"It's mainly guys sticking wire brushes down pipes and using customer-provided compressed air to clear vents." I smiled, thinking about the simplicity of such a profitable business.

Bill shepherded the call forward. "Josh noticed how the pumping business is growing, and how they are getting into water jetting and doing more catch basins," he said. "Reid, those are both areas that we are looking to do more of."

"Those businesses are my favorite growth areas," I affirmed.

"You are asking a high price," Josh stated.

"The other option is an ESOP. I have the deal through credit," I said with authentic excitement. While employee ownership would be a challenge, I love a good challenge. If they turned this deal down, I was happy to do an ESOP.

"We have no interest in being part of that," Josh exclaimed.

"I know. It is an either-or," I said.

"OK. We are interested. We want to grow our company in your geography, and we think you have a strong business. Bill will be back in touch."

The call had gone well. I had been honest, established the ESOP as my alternative, and hadn't said anything stupid. I called Dan (a peer group operator friend) to recap and was then back to the daily grind. That was my first diligence call with such a high-caliber individual—the CEO of a private-equity-backed, 800-employee company. I had done well. Preparation, honesty, and positivity had paid off. It was a step forward in a 1,000-mile journey. Josh and Bill would be coming to visit in a few weeks.

When selling one of my fitness clubs, I was proactive in providing information early in the process. Putting myself in the buyer's shoes, I provided all the information I would want to know: financials since the club opened ten years prior, remittance statements since the beginning, attrition rates, the lease, and everything else on the diligence list. The buyer did not make any additional diligence requests, and the sale closed at my asking price. While there are legitimate concerns about providing information to certain buyers, such as competitors, being prepared with the information you need before it is requested will help move the sale forward and avoid the perception that you are withholding information.

Keep It Simple: Signed LOI

On March 15, the LOI for the industrial services business was signed at the asking price, with a three-month transition for me. The buyer had discussed my staying on longer, but I did not envision myself being an employee. I wanted an all-cash deal. I prefer simplicity. I recently witnessed the sellers of a healthcare company caught up in a costly lawsuit with the buyer about the value of rolled equity (when the seller retains partial ownership in the company). While the outcome ended fairly given the circumstances, and the legal fees were covered by the non-prevailing party, the opportunity cost of the time spent fighting couldn't be recovered. Even in the absence of a lawsuit, accountants and attorneys often have to be engaged to calculate the numbers and trade correspondence back and forth before a price is agreed to, all at a cost of thousands of dollars.

There is an argument to be made that rolling equity has tremendous value, especially if, as an EBO, you believe in the vision of the acquirer. A personal services EBO I know who sold to a private equity firm rolled equity and is happy he did. He describes the key to the relationship being that the acquirer values his opinion about the business operations even if they do not follow his advice. As my academic research shows, as a seller the key is to have a values-based vision for your role post sale and take intentional action to achieve it.[26]

Optimize Timing: Anchor High

When we signed the LOI in mid-March, we negotiated over a target close date. I remember thinking that six weeks was more than enough time. The buyer eventually agreed on the end of May, which they thought was aggressive. To me, ten weeks seemed easy. With focus, I knew we could hit that with no problem. I am a proponent of setting lofty goals and then pushing to hit them. Even if they are missed, by making progress toward them, we end up better off. I was determined to hit the ten weeks and would do everything in my control to make it

26 | www.reidtileston.com

happen. Responding in a timely manner to diligence requests, such as the forty-three-page diligence checklist, was a critical step in that process. Countless intermediaries and EBOs know that time kills deals. Matt Jones, an intermediary I have worked with, sums it up with the saying, "Time is enemy #1."

How to Handle Tough Decisions: Be Honest

I created and advertised the shared vision of having the smoothest business sale in the history of the world. Commensurate with this goal was not having any lawsuits. I value honesty above all. The truth always comes out, and the sooner it does, the better. It is necessary, however, to negotiate legal considerations such as liability caps. There is no reason to take on risk. Legal protection is of secondary importance. Brutal honesty is best.

When it came time to fill out a legal disclosure list, I enumerated every shortcut we had ever taken. It was a gut-wrenching experience. I wanted everything out there. The fact that I was using a waste profile from one customer to offload waste from another at the landfill and the six times we had pumped water from a decontamination tank at a hospital and classified it as grease when offloading made the cut—I revealed it all. The business was well run; however, painful as it is to say, it was not perfect. The flip side of this is being too honest. We had had a bad showing with a top customer; they were not happy. The customer was planning on getting competitive bids for future work. Did this need to be disclosed? I thought yes. Everyone else told me no. It was not material, and it was business as usual; the bad showings there were a tradition for us, and getting competitive bids was normal.

"Disclosing that will needlessly throw a wrench in things. It will also take up attorney time as they dig into it," a business peer group EBO friend told me.

This speaks again to my peer groups saving me from myself. In the absence of their guidance, I would have disclosed, disclosed, and disclosed to no one's benefit. Had I done this enough, I could have killed the deal. As it turned out, the customer ended up placing the usual order with us anyway, with a few additions, and we completed it as usual. The job also included a significant price hike to make sure we could properly staff the job to minimize the chance of service issues. The service was completed without incident, and the customer paid on time. This was no surprise, given they have been a customer for over thirty-five years.

Disclosing during diligence will help avoid costly disputes post-close and lead to a smoother transition. An EBO who sold her niche commercial services business with a well executed transition said, "Going above and beyond during diligence is critical to the success of the transition."

How To Maximize Leverage: Performance and Alternatives Pay

The agreed-to purchase price was based on previous years' numbers. In the current year, however, the business had grown by 24.61 percent in January, 58.25 percent in February, 44.94 percent in March, 19.59 percent in April, and 18.96 percent in May. Overall, revenue growth would clock in at 31.88 percent during the time we agreed on the purchase price to close. The profit margins had also improved, in addition to the top-line revenue. I thought the purchase price was already rich, but my peer groups told me otherwise. While I could have asked for a higher price based on the increased performance, I chose to honor our original agreement. It was the right thing to do.

Three years earlier, when I was conducting diligence on buying the business, Dan, a peer group friend, had called National Pumping (the buyer) to ask them how they would think about valuing a company like the one I was looking at. The buyer mostly kept their cards close to their chest, yet they gave away two pieces of critical information: 1) they were attracted to companies like this; and 2) they deducted from the purchase the cost of any trucks that needed to be replaced. I knew this might be coming. The buyer did not disappoint.

"We should have done this earlier," Bill said. "I was talking with Jack, and we are going to need to deduct the price of the truck that you have on order from the purchase price, as it is a capital expense."

Rich had recently told me that a smart strategy when responding to a ridiculous request, this request being ridiculous because it should have been addressed earlier when we were negotiating the terms of the deal, is to go crazy and then return to calm once the situation has returned to the status quo.

I responded from the gray area between speaking and yelling: "I agreed to the purchase price, and the business has been doing even better during the last few months. I will follow through on my commitment to stick to our original purchase price, even though I may be able to get more money, because it is the right thing to do. If you want to re-trade, then we can reanalyze performance, and I'll increase the purchase price. Otherwise, I am going to do the ESOP."

"Why don't I set up a call with you and Jack to discuss?" Bill asked.

"We can do a call, but I am just going to tell him the exact same thing," I said.

The request was withdrawn the next day, and the deal moved forward. Knowing that this ask might come minimized the emotional impact. Having the leverage of the fact that the business was crushing it, coupled with a viable alternative for an exit, gave me the tools to navigate issues as we approached the finish line. Kudos to Rich for giving me awesome and pragmatic advice.

While strong performance is an EBO's best leverage, one advantage to using an intermediary is that they often will have a formal back-up offer in place to use as leverage to move a deal forward. There are also more sophisticated strategies that I have seen used successfully, such as accepting LOIs from two competing buyers with instructions that the buyer that is quickest to finish diligence and has a signed sale agreement gets to move forward.

How to Create a Shared Vision

I had told the team about the sale, and the next day, two weeks before our planned closing date, the buyer was coming to town to meet the employees.

I kicked off the meeting: "Our goal is the smoothest transition in the history of business. The buyer and I both agree on the importance of you, the team, and we see eye to eye on the importance of paying retention bonuses. If not managed properly, transitions can be painful. Just like we did with Service Titan (our migration to the cloud), we are going to be thoughtful, and we are going to make this one of the smoothest acquisitions in the history of National Pumping. That starts today. Ask lots of questions. If you are even thinking it, ask it."

The buyer had done twenty-seven acquisitions. This was not their first rodeo. They came prepared. Jacob (their head of acquisitions), two HR representatives, and Jim (the newly hired assistant general manager) were in attendance to answer questions. They brought individual packets for each team member with promises to send engagement letters thereafter.

The buyer had initially asked me to wait until the transition meeting to inform team members of the sale. The idea was to do the transition meeting, conduct background screenings and HR paperwork, and then close two weeks later. I hated this idea with passion because

I saw no benefit to the team knowing about the sale before it was complete. I was willing to take the risk with the ESOP as the alternative option. I had talked to Jacob probably 100 times over the phone and Zoom. I wanted to meet him in person. I reached out to him and offered to meet him at his hotel the night before the buyer was going to meet the team.

Honesty is the only policy. I informed Jacob that I had told the team about the sale and retention bonuses. Jacob is a smooth operator; he took all this in stride, like he had heard it all before. First impressions matter, and I wanted the team members to bring their best foot forward for the meeting with the buyers to kick things off on the right foot. I did not have anything to hide; I was transparent about the good and the bad parts of the business. The more preparation for the meeting, the smoother it would be; the smoother the meeting, the higher chance of a smooth transition. A smoother transition would lead to a better outcome for the buyer, the team members, and me. Telling the team members was a no-brainer. Knowing that the buyer would be there, and my messaging around this buyer being the one willing to pay retention bonuses, would provide the needed fire.

Jacob had quite the poker face. He responded without emotion. I updated him on the rest of the happenings; it was all business-as-usual news. Tom was on board, one of the trucks just got fixed, Ruthless (our new truck driver to replace Taylor) was killing it, and everyone was tentatively excited about the meeting tomorrow.

I wanted Jacob to be prepared for the meeting as well. I emphasized that Tom was concerned about whether the buyer would restrict the work that the business did, and I also implored him in person (as I had via email with HR) to change the names on the offer letters from their legal names to the names they used on a day-to-day basis. Tom's letter was addressed "Dear Thomas." My guess is that Tom has never been referred to as Thomas in his entire life. Thoughtfulness counts. I could think of few worse ways to kick things off than with an impersonal touch. Unfortunately, the letters were not changed.

Transition meetings run the gamut from uneventful to emotionally fraught. An EBO who sold a specialized contracting business described his team members to the buyer as being "way more calm about it and laid back about it than I was." Another EBO had employees quit on the spot, only to reconsider a short time later.

How to Manage Key People: Control What You Can

An EBO who was selling a manufacturing business who kept his employees in the loop about the sale; after all, they had minor equity stakes, and the EBO wanted to be open with them as he had always been. The team members ended up slowing the sale because they wanted more equity. They eventually came to an agreement, but this led to a toxic relationship between seller and buyer. The team members who led this charge did not last long after the sale, and the seller later expressed regret over how the incident was handled. On the flip side, another EBO who sold a niche commercial services business told the employees he intended to sell and successfully navigated the deal to close without any issues and minimal post-close attrition. Secrecy is a significant cause of stress for sellers. Tread carefully.

With the industrial services business, I was not given the option— the key employee conversation was with Tom. I was going with the assumptive close. This was going to be his fourth sale. I had learned to expect the unexpected with Tom. I was ready for anything.

"Tom, I am selling the business. You know the buyer: National Pumping. We see eye to eye on the importance of the team members, so you and the rest of the team will be getting a retention bonus. I am going to tell the team later today as they come in," I stated matter-of-factly, just as Rich from my peer group had coached me.

At this point, I had taken up the habit of standing when I talked to Tom. This was to even the power dynamic of our height difference, since he was often standing as well.

"I knew it. All those meetings were the giveaway," he said. "National Pumping is a bunch of clowns."

I wanted to laugh; Tom always has a classic comment up his sleeve.

"What are you going to do?" he inquired.

"Focus on making this the smoothest transition in the history of business sales in the short term and then pursue other endeavors," I said. "They will be here tomorrow at 8:00 a.m. to meet the team, so come prepared with questions. Please keep this conversation to yourself until I have a chance to tell the team, which I am going to today as they trickle in."

Tom's countenance indicated he could handle this with one eye closed. Still, his previous three transitions were with individuals, whereas this was a strategic buyer. This was a different ballgame. While I thought Tom did not know what he was in for, he is adaptable, and I was confident he would adapt and thrive in his new environment.

There would be plenty of surprises for us both as the next two weeks played out.

Meeting the buyer was a tough day for Tom. During their one-on-one meeting, Tom was concerned that the acquisition was about what the business could provide for the buyer, as opposed to what the buyer could do for the business. In addition to addressing him as "Thomas," the offer letter put Tom's title as branch operations manager; Tom had last been the operations manager in the eighties. I did not realize the impact that this change of title would have on Tom; he would still be the one calling the shots, but the title stung. In addition, I had diligently run the numbers months ago to illustrate how Tom would be making more money with the buyer; Tom interpreted the numbers in his offer letter as adding up to less than he was currently making. It wasn't the case, and I had a spreadsheet to prove it, but it didn't help the first impressions. To add more bad news, his pay was moving from bi-weekly to weekly, which would throw a wrench in how he and his wife managed cash flow.

Tom had the somber realization that this buyer was a different kind of beast. He was the experienced team captain; he was responsible for keeping everyone else cool. The team captain having a meltdown was not part of the equation.

Tom expressed his frustration to me in no uncertain terms. "I do not like that Jacob guy."

Unfortunately for Jacob, Tom had decided to sum up his negative feelings about the entire situation and center them on Jacob. Better him than me! It was not clear to me what Tom was going to do. It was going to be an exciting and stress-filled next two weeks to close. The ball was in Tom's court. Other team members got the impression that it was a done deal; Tom knew he could still kill it. I phoned a peer group friend to vent and ask for advice.

"Should I tell Tom about the ESOP?" I asked.

"Do you think he will prefer the ESOP to the buyer?" he asked.

"Yes. I think he would rather me stick around and push forward the ESOP," I responded, proud of myself for mustering up the courage to be honest with myself.

"Then do not tell him! It is like you are trying to kill the deal. You deserve this," he said after a short silence for effect. Once again, a strategic advisor saved me from myself.

The next day, Tom came in with a few declarations.

"I am not going to kill your deal," he said. This was music to my ears, because Tom had followed through on every promise he had ever made to me. My gut feeling was that as long as the buyer did not do anything monumentally stupid, the deal would happen. I could feel the serotonin and dopamine flowing through my veins, and happiness ensued.

With Tom's high-level declaration that he was not going to kill the deal, I felt more confident. I knew challenges lay ahead. My focus was on getting the deal closed, knowing my alternative was the ESOP.

Tom continued with the negotiations around his salary, responsibility, and title. I was in a challenging place. I was still the owner of the business, and the buck stopped with me. Yet I wanted to project an air of confidence that the deal was going to close with 100 percent certainty. I was in a state of boss-not-boss. I resolved to show unrivaled mental strength and operate with complete authority, like nothing had changed.

My heartache continued as Tom and the buyer negotiated. He got a raise, detailed out his responsibilities, and they worked through the non-compete. I did my best to stay unbiased in these conversations and let Tom work with the buyer directly. As boss-not-boss, I was soon to be out of the picture. I only interjected when I knew I could add value. I had my attorney review the non-compete and provide Tom feedback in real time to avoid having to wait for a third party. It was a delicate balance. I wanted to get the deal closed, and I also recognized that Tom had to do what was best for him.

Eventually, Tom signed the non-compete and employment agreement. He was resigned to the fact that the business would have a fourth owner. The elation of the weight being lifted from my chest was enormous.

Having the ESOP as an alternative was key. With one issue re-solved, there were still plenty of challenges yet to come.

Move Fast: There Is No Time Like the Present

Despite my positive conversation with Tom, Bill and Josh were con-cerned that Tom might leave if they decided to let any of the exist-ing team members go. They had a policy against hiring people with a criminal background but had agreed to keep on existing team mem-bers unless any problems arose. They knew how close Tom was to ev-eryone on the team.

"Tom is important," Bill and Josh said. "We are concerned what will happen if we are forced to let a team member go. Will Tom con-tinue to stick around, given how close he is to certain team members?"

"I don't think it will be a problem. Let's go to the horse's mouth. I will head back to the shop, and let's get Tom on the phone. Just ask him."

"I'm working from home and heading to the grocery store, but I can make that work," Josh responded, surprised by my candor and urgency.

I got back to the shop ten minutes later. When Tom got on the phone, I told him to be honest and ask whatever questions he had. Tom, Bill, and Josh had their conversation, with me as the intermedi-ary. Tom said it would not be a problem and asked them about their plans for the business. Bill and Josh responded like slick executives of-ten do, optimistic and non-committal throughout.

"Did Tom allay your concerns? I asked.

"Yes," Josh replied.

"Tom, do you have any additional concerns you would like to dis-cuss?" I asked.

"I'm good," he said.

As opposed to losing sleep and increasing stress, I took the bull by the horns and addressed the issue. I was quick with assessment and focused on forward momentum. Had it been a deal breaker, I wanted to know sooner rather than later so I could move on.

How to Manage a Lease Assignment

It is critical to work with the decision-maker—in this case, the landlord of the property. We were a week and a half away from our close date of May 31. The buyer was taking over the property lease, and it was necessary to work with the landlord to process the lease assignment to the buyer. The buyer had sent a lease assignment to the landlord a few weeks prior. During the sale, I made sure we were on track. I was reminded of something that the buyer's in-house counsel said: "We always find a way to get these things done on time." *Interesting,* I thought. *I guess I am in for quite a ride. Hopefully it ends well!*

The landlord's representative had ignored the assignment; when I followed up with him, he acknowledged it and agreed to a call. He came completely unprepared; the buyers' in-house counsel, their outside counsel real estate guy, and their contract lead were on the phone ready to go through the document. The call was a waste of time.

I had never had to deal with the landlord directly during my own lease assignment when I purchased the business. Yet he was the decision-maker, and with time ticking to our close deadline, I went directly to him. With a bit of scrappiness, I found his cellphone number online and reached out to him. He gave me an angry earful about how the buyer was acting like an 800-pound gorilla. I pointed out that it was a win-win deal, and he was the only blocker. He asked me to pay his attorney's fees because no attorney would be necessary if the buyer

agreed to the assignment at the current terms without trying to negotiate a new lease. I said I would do that if the document was signed in
the next three days.

In getting real estate deals done, it is a rite of passage to have at
least one shouting match with the landlord. I understood both perspectives and was more in line with the landlord. He was being forced
to deal with a difficult new tenant.

I am a stickler for deadlines. We were set to close on Tuesday, May
31—the day after Memorial Day. I figured out who their attorney was,
reached out to her, and requested that she agree to a call before the
long weekend. I was not going to let this deal get held up by landlords
and attorneys. To her credit, she did agree to a call, and I attended as
a fly on the wall to monitor. It was forty-five minutes of billable hours
around a slew of complex legal terms. The end result was a layman's
discussion-level agreement that we were going to assign the current
lease and revisit when the option term came up—a reasonable solution all parties were on board with. However, it was Friday, and the
landlord was going on vacation for Memorial Day weekend and would
not be available to sign until he returned, which would push back
our close.

I personally took responsibility and sent the landlord the document via DocuSign along with a plethora of follow-up calls and
emails. A quick answer was critical, as travel schedules needed to be
confirmed for Tuesday. I was intent on pushing this forward. I chose
to be positive and made the assumptive close.

On Saturday morning, the landlord sent back the signed form
from vacation. Happy Saturday. We were a go for Tuesday. I was starting to get cautiously optimistic that this was going to happen. While
I have seen deals fall apart all the way up to the second before close,

things were certainly moving in the right direction. Being proactive paid off.

While being proactive is good, the best cure is prevention. When negotiating real estate leases, I attempt to give the landlord no right to refuse a buyer. I sold a fitness club where the landlord was given the right to review the buyer but had no authority to prevent a transfer, which was one less thing to worry about.

Crossing the Finish Line

Monday, May 30 was a great day. The high-rise where I lived had a nice pool, and Memorial Day was a prime time to enjoy it. The weather was beautiful, and friends of mine from running club were at the pool enjoying the sun and scene. As had been the case for the last three years, I was upstairs creating economic value. I was determined to be all-in until the end. The buyer's attorneys and I were going back and forth on the signature pages for the purchase agreement. My attorney had stepped up and gotten the final changes in. I was reading, rereading, and eventually signing. With all the chaos leading up to close, it is easy to make mistakes. But mistakes can be costly! I did my best to make sure every exhibit, disclosure, schedule, and such was where it needed to be. I did not notice any mistakes. I know from experience that there are always mistakes; it is just a matter of looking hard enough.

Sure enough, the mistake was in the flow of funds; they had allocated the wrong amount to my lender. The mistake was caught and revised. Catching the mistake had undoubtedly saved me hours in the future.

I got a text from the buyer revisiting the issue of the truck; there was a deposit I had paid months ago. While they had dropped that issue, they were not willing to give me the deposit back. While I think it should have been re-credited, I was willing to bite the bullet on that one.

I take pride in the fact that on a national holiday, there were seven people working to push the American economy forward. The harder the country works, the luckier the country is going to get.

"How are you doing, Reid?" their attorney asked me.

"I'm good. Excited we are pushing this forward on a holiday. The weather is beautiful here," I said.

"We have a bad weather front up here; we will send it your way shortly," he responded.

Leave it to an attorney to kill the fun by being the bearer of bad news. All the documents were signed. We were as ready as could be to close the following day.

The Day of Close

I was getting sentimental. I was reflecting on how much I loved the grit-it-done culture of the company. The transition meeting started at 7:00 a.m., a late start for a company where the trucks typically start rolling around 5:00 a.m. I had a closing check-in call at 8:00 a.m., and the formal closing was set to happen at 10:45 a.m. For nearly three hours, I was stuck in purgatory with my serious sales hat on during the transition meeting, concerned that at any moment a blow-up of some kind might occur.

At 10:45 a.m., I strolled to my office for the official closing call. There were about a dozen team members and service providers (probably charging hourly) there. After a brief delay, Josh joined the call.

Trent, a third-party attorney asked, "Are you ready to finalize the close?"

"Yes," I answered .

Josh stated, "Yes."

The attorney pronounced, "We are closed. Congratulations!"

This was miracle #1. Miracle #2 would come a few hours later when the money was transferred to my bank account. Thankfully, it was!

The Day After

The business sale is not the end of the journey. Once the deal closes, the transition begins. Transitions typically last between a few weeks and a few years. I did not pay lip service to having the smoothest transition in history. The next day, I was back, cranking it out, starting with my 8:00 a.m. meeting with Marylin. A good portion of the buyer's team had stayed over to ensure that business as usual was being executed.

There is a lot to do during a transition. I think that true character is not how someone starts a relationship but how they end it. I was determined to do the right thing at every turn.

How to Handle a Transition

I have observed a lot of painful business transitions. A leading reason is often the inherently awkward relationship between the buyer and the seller after closing. In fact, Stanford publishes an annual study, and they cite the relationship between the buyer and seller as being a leading reason behind under-performing acquisitions.[27] Whether it's fights over the value of rolled equity, true-ups about who covered what expenses, legal disputes, bitterness about the direction of the company, or just plain anger about being around post-close and having to work, the relationships between buyer and seller often sours. The seller is in an interesting position. The hard authority is gone, but soft authority remains. A clean, vision-based exit is my personal preference.

27 | Peter Kelly & Sarah Heston, "2022 Search Fund Study: Selected Observations, Graduate School of Stanford Business, 2022, gsb.stanford.edu/faculty-research/case-studies/2022-search-fund-study-selected-observations

A logistics firm seller I know was under contract to stick around for a year post-sale to complete a transition and help the incoming leader. After about a month, he was clearly upset to be there even though he was getting paid. He spent most of his time reconciling what expenses he was owed, the value of his retained equity, and being a critical naysayer. While there was no lawsuit, his presence was detrimental. He was eventually terminated from his transition role but not before damage was done.

On the flip side, one seller of a distribution business who took 100 percent cash still goes by the business to get lunch with the owner and team members about once a month, even though it is a few hours from where he lives and his transition period is over. It is an open-arms relationship that all parties are happy with. Even with all-cash deals, the buyer can still sue the seller, so having an open relationship where the seller is available and helpful is a smart best practice.

Follow Through

I appreciated that the buyer and the team allowed me to enjoy my trip to Niesen. Marylin, being her usual organized and proactive self, had booked a vacation for the last week of June and given me ample notice. With enough foresight, anything can be accomplished and accommodated. As an economics professor once pointed out to me, "In the long run, everything is elastic." Even in the midst of a sale and transition, because her vacation was planned for, it would happen and business as usual would be uninterrupted.

I promised I was going to cover for Marylin when she was on vacation. I did her job for the week. Even though I was no longer the owner, I acted exactly the way I would have if I had been: raising prices for difficult customers, working to cut out red tape associated with doing work for Fortune 500 companies, putting together grease-trap runs, and, of course, setting up service agreements.

An EBO seller I worked with was hungry to get out of the business as quickly as possible to focus on his family, and he made this clear during the sale process. The EBO buyer ultimately won the deal by offering a short but intense transition with a thorough and aggressive, yet achievable, to-do list that was crafted in advance of close. It worked out well because both parties stuck to their commitments and had a successful transition, even though the buyer had no previous experience in the space.

A Smooth End

Less than a month after closing, I would never set foot inside the business again. At the end of February, I had started conversations with the strategic buyer. We had a signed LOI in the middle of March, we closed at the end of May, and I was out of the picture by the end of June. At the time of writing, everyone is happy. The retention bonuses were paid; I got paid, and the business is doing well.

Do the Right Thing

My peer group friend Dan was there for me every step of the way while closing the deal. Whenever I needed strategic advice or simply a shoulder to cry on, he was a phone call away. A few days after close and without being asked, I wrote him a nice check and begged him to cash it to monetize my appreciation. Money talks! In addition, I spent a lot of one bank's time and money chasing down the ESOP deal. One banker in particular went above and beyond for me. I offered to pay him a commission out of respect for his time. He respectfully declined the gesture. I am hopeful that he learned from the experience and can do some SBA 7a ESOP deals in the future to get a return on the time invested.

If anyone reading this book is interested in an SBA 7a ESOP deal, please reach out to me at reid@grititdone.com. I will point you in the right direction. Employee ownership is a noble cause, and I hope you can benefit from the hard work that we both put into structuring the deal. The ESOP regulations make the process harder than it needs to be, and there is no need to relive our pain by reinventing the wheel.

Keep It Simple

My advice to readers of this book is, for the good of the country, strive to keep it simple when conducting transactions. Avoid profiting from the gray area, and own your actions. We can do better than we currently are. Business cannot progress until all Is are dotted and Ts crossed. As a society, we bear the costs. The cost is not only money but also time. Time is the ultimate commodity. I promise myself that, on the other side, I will take action to improve the political and regulatory system for the benefit of our country.

Synopsis

Go all-in and enjoy the journey! I feel tremendous pride about the people projects. It was challenging, but at the end of the day, I feel proud that I did my part to push the team members to be better than when they entered my life. I sleep well at night, and so will you! I am reminded to be thankful for all of my peers who have pushed me to be better.

Next Step

I hope you have enjoyed reading this as much as I have enjoyed writing it. EBOs make better citizens, and I encourage everyone to take the plunge. Continue the conversation by visiting www.reidtileston.com/grititdone.

CONCLUSION

The general advice in the entrepreneurial business ownership space is to take six months off post-close, do nothing, and figure out your next steps. I prefer to enjoy the view from the top and then quickly move onto the next challenge.

After I finished Niesen-Treppenlauf, I completed a few other endurance events, including a Rim-to-Rim hike of the Grand Canyon in a day, the Presidential Traverse in New Hampshire in a day, swimming in Antarctica, and doing a lap around the world. A few weeks after close, I applied and was admitted to a doctoral program at Case Western to study Entrepreneurship Through Acquisition, and shortly thereafter I embarked upon writing this book and teaching this material as an adjunct professor at Case Western. The country is made better with more EBOs, and it is my pleasure to encourage as many individuals as possible down the path.

You picked up this book because you were interested in low-risk business ownership, and now you have gone through the nine steps that will help you accomplish that. You started this book yearning for autonomy, to control your calendar, and to own the upside of your work, yet you were held back by fear and uncertainty. You now have a road map that will minimize your risk.

The choice is yours: either stay the course or take the plunge into entrepreneurial business ownership by pursuing a fundamental business with a grit-it-done attitude. If you do, you will feel the elation, ecstasy, and excitement of being all-in.

ACKNOWLEDGMENTS

I would like to thank my grandmother, mother, and father for all writing books setting the groundwork for me to follow.

I would also like to thank Trevor and Zac for getting me started in my small business career during our fateful night at Old Ship Saloon on Battery Street in San Francisco.

To Gwen for running Anytime Fitness Winters while I explored life in the Midwest and for sticking by my side through all my life endeavors.

Thank you to Mark Agnew and Brian O'Connor for agreeing to add a second TA to the inaugural Entrepreneurship Through Acquisition class at Booth in 2015. Being the TA of that class was transformational for my career.

It is not fair to mention Booth without mentioning Alex Hodgkin who, with his vision, energy, and persistence, took the bull by the horns and has been critical in building Booth Entrepreneurship Through Acquisition into what it is today.

Thank you to Scot Lowry, Simon Peck, and the rest of the Entrepreneurship Through Acquisition community at Case Western for their support.

Thank you to all of my forum mates for your mentorship and guidance.

None of this would have been possible without Dan; failure is the building block for success, my friend.

Thanks to Walker Deibel, Richard Ruback, Royce Yudkoff, and Jan Simon for writing books that have continued the collaborative spirit that the community was founded and built upon by Jim Southern and Irv Grousbeck. I am honored to add to the literature with this writing.

I have John Pickerel to thank for teaching me at a young age that true fulfillment from business ownership comes from improving lives.

Lastly, this book is dedicated to all the past, present, and future EBOs out there who are on the ground doing the real work.

www.ingramcontent.com/pod-product-compliance
Lightning Source LLC
Chambersburg PA
CBHW071217090426
42736CB00014B/2865